tales of a driftwood

tales of a driftwood

recollections of mostly unplanned travel
gangadharan menon

PARTRIDGE

To order additional copies of this book, contact
Partridge India
000 800 10062 62
orders.india@partridgepublishing.com

www.partridgepublishing.com/india

To Arundhati, my granddaughter, and all the little children from whom we have borrowed the Earth.

This Book is about the joys of travel. But it is not a 'How to' Book. It doesn't tell you How to Get There, Where to Stay, and When to Go. Instead, it's about exploring the world, and the joy of mostly unplanned travel. It's about what these journeys have done to me. How they have made me. So in that sense, it's private, it's introspective.

A good traveller has no fixed plans, and is not intent on arriving.

—*Lao Tzu*

I haven't been everywhere, but it's on my list.

—*Susan Sontag*

Travelling leaves you speechless. Then it turns you into a storyteller.

—*Ibn Batuta*

Contents

the golden temple of jejuri

Rajani, the Goddess of Night, had the complexion of night. She always wondered what she would look like if she had the complexion of the morning sun. Mustering courage to ask for the impossible, she climbed up to Mount Kailas. Prostrating at Shiva's feet, she told him, 'Lord, I am an unfortunate soul who's forever dark. Could you bless me with a golden hue?' Shiva was in a jovial and generous mood. Instantly he blessed her and said, 'Your dream will come true. Go and lie down on top of Mount Skanda. After a while, you will disappear into the womb of Mother Earth and will be reborn as the turmeric plant that has the complexion of molten sun. You will become the symbol of purity and auspiciousness. And when I descend on Earth as Khandoba, my favourite offering will be the powder of turmeric.'

As you walk up the hillock of Jejuri, you will find yellow clouds of turmeric wafting in the air and softly landing on the 200 stone steps that lead you to Khandoba, the lord of the tribals.

Jejuri is situated 50 kilometres to the south-east of Pune and is the abode of the lord of the oldest tribe in Maharashtra, the dhangars. They are an upright and valiant community of shepherds, and they are deeply attached to Khandoba as he had married Ganai, the daughter of a shepherd.

There's a paradox about Khandoba. He has two wives: One is a goddess and the other is a shepherd's daughter. In spite of this blatant bigamy, couples throng here soon after marriage seeking a long and happy married life. And incidentally Jejuri is the only temple where a couple has to make the offering to the deity together standing next to each other.

One of the main visual attractions of Jejuri is the deepmaala, or the garland of lights. There are two of them: tall, vertical columns carved in black stone. When lit up all at once on a moonless night, the shimmering flood of light created by these stone garlands is enough to rival the molten gold of turmeric that forever adorns the steps of Jejuri.

There are ritual songs sung by traditional families, on request, for the fertility of newly married couples. Armed with an ektaara, and blessed with a rustic voice, they sing without inhibition – praying for the marital bliss of couples.

But Khandoba, despite his demeanour of an easily appeased lord, is actually an angry incarnation of Lord Shiva who descended on Earth to slay two demons, Mani and Malla. He has an interesting martial symbol. It's called divti. It's shaped like a dagger, but doubles up as a lamp. So when it's lit up it looks like a flaming dagger: a symbol of light that slays darkness.

Jejuri is now a temple; but once upon a time it was a fort. A historic one at that because it's here that Shivaji met his father Shahaji after a long gap of 14 years, and discussed guerilla strategies to fight the Mughals.

The temple that you see now is the new temple. The old one that inspired Arun Kolatkar to write the Commonwealth-Poetry-Prize-Winning 'Jejuri' is situated atop a hill three kilometres away. Describing the dilapidated condition of this temple like only he could, Arun wrote:

'That's no doorstep.

It's a pillar on its side.

Yes.

That's what it is.'

There's a fascinating story about how the old temple moved to the new location. Many many years ago, you had to undertake an arduous climb to reach the old temple. One of Khandoba's devotees had been doing that daily for over 50 years. One day, he realized that his mind is willing but his body couldn't take it anymore. So he bid goodbye to Khandoba, saying it was his last visit to the temple. The lord was touched by the words of his ardent devotee and he told him: 'Since you can't come to see me, I will come with you and live in your house. But on one condition: you shouldn't turn back to look at me when I'm following you. If you do, I will stop right there'. The old man's joy knew no bounds and he readily agreed. And the lord started following him. The old man thought to himself: 'The lord has asked me not to look at him, but I can always keep an ear open for the lord's footfalls'. But after a while the footfalls stopped. Fearing that the lord had lost his way, he turned back. The lord froze into stone then and there, and a new temple was built around that idol.

Looking down from the temple you see the Kaara river into which Khandoba descends to take a cool dip on the moonless night of Somvati Amaavasya.

On that day, the joy of the devotees is a little more than ever. They sprinkle a little more turmeric powder than ever; and the steps of Jejuri become a little more golden than ever.

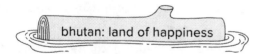

bhutan: land of happiness

There's a beautiful folktale in Bhutan. It is drawn on the walls of their houses and their monasteries as a constant reminder of the Bhutanese Way of Life. Illustrated in the Tibetan Buddhist style, it shows an elephant standing under a fruit-laden tree. On its back is a monkey on whose back is a rabbit on whose back is a bird. The story goes like this: Once a hungry elephant came to a tree to pluck its fruits. A monkey came running and said, 'Stop, I have the first right to these fruits as I guarded this tree ever since it started bearing fruit.' Just as he jumped on to the elephant's back to pluck the fruits, a rabbit came scurrying and said, 'Hey you guys, I have the first right as I protected this tree as a sapling and prevented the cattle from nibbling at it'. And as the rabbit jumped on to the monkey's back, a bird flew down and landed on the rabbit's shoulders and said, 'You may have all looked after the tree in its various stages of growth, but I was the one who brought the seed here in the first place. So let's all share it and give some to our big friend, the elephant.' Truly a wonderful food chain where all living things are treated as equal.

The Bhutanese respect all that dwells in Nature. According to law, 60% of their land has always to be covered with forest. That figure stands at a healthy 72% today, thanks to the Forest Day on 2nd December when every year they plant tens of thousands of trees on their hill slopes, across the country.

The drive from Paro, along the blue-green Pa Chu river, was a visual delight. There were pine trees, cypress trees, deodar trees, willow trees and maple trees. And there were yellow trees, orange trees, red trees, green trees and pink trees. The maple trees were looking the most stunning wearing just leaves of sunlight.

The riot of colour continues in their culture too. There were white manider flags that were strung together on poles to pray for dear departed souls, and the 5-colour lungta festoons for granting of wishes. All along the innumerable passes you would find them fluttering in the breeze as the Bhutanese believe it's the wind that carries your prayers to God.

The Bhutanese, being predominantly Buddhist, revere all things living. So felling of trees (even if they belong to you, permission has to be sought to cut them), hunting of animals (though archery is their national sport), and even fishing for commerce, is a no-no. This extends interestingly even to inanimate objects. Mountaineering is prohibited in the whole of Bhutan as the tall mountains are held in high esteem. The Bhutanese believe that opening up these pristine mountains to humans will only end up with the litter of civilization. The reported pollution along the neighbouring mountains of Nepal and India have only made their resolve that much stronger.

The next day we woke up before the sun, and travelled faster than him to reach Dochu La for our first glimpse of the unconquered peaks of the Bhutan Himalayas. But when we reached there, we realized he was yet to reach there. And we froze at -4 degrees C. Some cameras got jammed, and my fingers too froze just as I focussed on the frozen peaks in the distance.

Slowly the sun appeared and melted our frozen moments, making us realize the importance of the life-giving sun in the neck of these cypress woods.

We drove down to the Pobjikha valley: one of the only five valleys in Bhutan, the rest being mountains stitched by roads. As we descended, I was told by our friend, philosopher and guide Tashey that there's a unique law in Bhutan that insists that all houses must follow the Bhutanese architecture or else face a heavy penalty. The result was there for us to see. Beautiful houses built into the mountains that looked uniform yet individualistic. And I compared it with the houses in my homeland where great heritage architecture has been summarily replaced with concrete monstrosities.

Reaching Pobjikha by dusk we saw the last of the endangered blacknecked cranes settling down to roost for the night. As I looked at them landing on the dry riverbed, I remembered what Tashey had told me a while ago. These migratory birds, when they first come into Pobjikha, encircle the ancient monastery and then, only then, land on this riverbed. Every year. This could be explained away saying they are surveying the place to make sure it's safe to land. But they even fly around the monastery one last time before they fly back to the land of their birth. What explains that?

There's also the romantic story of a male blacknecked crane that stayed back to look after his injured girlfriend. It was only after she got enough strength in her wings a year later that the couple flew off to faraway lands. Talk about pairing for life.

In the morning we drove to Trongsa through Gangtey Pass. En route we stopped at Tashiling, the Land of the Melodious Water. Legend has it that the presiding deity of the mountain here fell in love with the beautiful daughter of a local farmer. In exchange for her hand he was willing to give away anything. Since there was no source of water here, all that the farmer asked for was water, the very source of life. And hey presto, a spring started gushing through the crevices. It is believed that anyone who drinks this water will have a melodious voice. The empirical evidence are the villagers here all of whom are excellent singers. Next to the spring is a giant Buddhist prayer-wheel that is being turned perennially by a gentle stream. When I saw the smiling eyes, young and old, near that spring I realized why the King of Bhutan always talks about Gross National Happiness. The Bhutanese are a happy lot, content with what they have. And this belief is so deep-rooted that they are the only country in the world to have an International Day of Happiness which is celebrated on the 20th of March every year.

It's a country that has no crime, and almost no corruption. They love their King and their Queen, and have their pictures put up at every home and every shop. Taking advantage of this, the King appears in one of the posters stating in unequivocal terms: 'I am not corrupt; and I will not tolerate corruption.' Imagine a single political leader in our country with this courage of conviction. As they say in Sanskrit: Yatha raja, tatha praja. The commoners imitate the king. This aspect is also reflected in their national dress. Proudly the royalty wears it; and so do the people.

Our last trip was to the highest pass in our journey: Chele La at 13,000 feet. We heard on the radio that the temperature the previous night was a comfortable -6 degrees C! So promptly all of us wore four layers of clothing and set off in the wee hours of the morning. Soon, the yonder snowclad peaks flashed past our windows playing hide and seek behind the pine trees. But when we landed at the pass it was absolutely comfortable. And I realised the fear of cold is sometimes worse that the cold itself.

Here we set off on the hunt for the elusive Himalayan monal. A bird that migrates from very high altitudes and comes lower down in search of warmth. Interestingly, they don't fly when they migrate. But merely walk down the slopes.

En route we saw rhododendrons, with only memories of a colourful yesterday clinging on to the dead branches.

There was a waterfall too. And at the bottom of it was a small rainbow. Being close by, I did look for the proverbial pot of gold at the end of the rainbow; but in vain.

Though we were looking for the elusive monal, what we saw was a small, nuclear family of the blood pheasant. A bird that looks like its neck has been sliced, and is bleeding profusely.

11

The blood reminded me of another legend of Bhutan, Drukpa Kuenly. He was a Buddhist monk known popularly as the Divine Madman. Sitting in Tibet, in the year 1499 to be precise, he shot an arrow from his bow and it landed in Bhutan. Following his nose and his arrow he landed here and proclaimed himself to be a Buddhist Lama. When the King asked him to show his resume,' he asked the King to bring him a dead goat and a dead cow. And he ceremoniously joined the head of the dead goat to the body of the dead cow, and hey presto the strange animal started walking. The descendants of this animal still walk the mountain slopes of Bhutan and is their national animal, Yakin.

On the last leg of our eventful journey, we passed by the mighty Mangde Chu river where they are planning to build a massive hydroelectric project to generate electricity that will be exported to India. The blasting at the site rang death knells in my head. So did the acts of sand dredging, illegal tree felling, and manmade forest fires that we witnessed sporadically in our one-week stay in this land of happiness.

Bhutan is blessed, as far as land to people ratio is concerned. In a land mass that's equal to the state of Kerala, they have just 7 lakh people as against the 3 crore population in Kerala. Will increase in population, and an all-consuming human greed, result in the loss of this paradise?

Only time will tell. Meanwhile, celebrate the joy of living with the most joyful humans on earth.

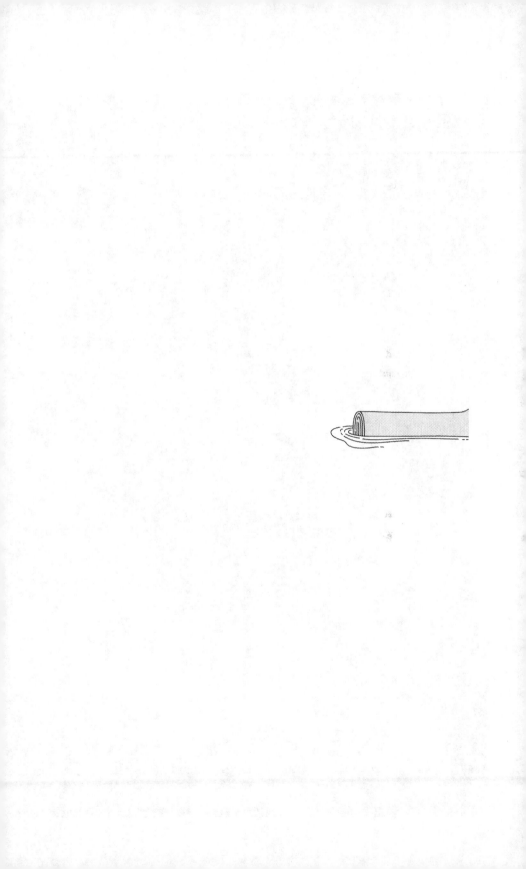

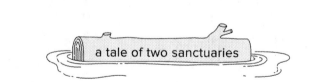

a tale of two sanctuaries

What's now Orang National Park was a densely populated tribal village around a hundred years ago. But the villagers deserted their homes en masse when a virulent epidemic called Black Fever struck their village; and they never returned. Over the next hundred years Nature healed herself, tree by tree. And today Orang is one of the most beautiful sanctuaries in Assam, and has earned the sobriquet of Mini Kaziranga.

All along our drive from Guwahati, one could see a phenomenon that's unique to this state and the faraway state of Kerala. There were innumerable pukhuris or ponds here, one in every house. In Kerala, they are called kulams. But in both these states the ponds are steadily being filled to satisfy the greed for land. Little realizing it's these ancient ponds that maintain the water level in the nearby wells.

We passed by Mangaldoi, better known as the vegetable farm of Assam, and the farmlands stretched as far as the eye could see without a single tree to obstruct the view.

On the outskirts of Silbori village we saw a very intriguing sight. The school-going kids here had two distinct sets of uniform: one for Ahomis and another one for Bodos. An indication that ethnicity runs deep, painfully deep.

At the far end of this village was the gate to Orang National Park. And on the fringe of the forest was our abode for the day: Prashaanti Tourism Complex with a gallery view of the forest.

When we woke up, the forest was missing. Slowly the morning mist that enveloped the whole forest moved away, revealing it layer by layer. We drove through the mist, the driver steering the jeep more by instinct than by sight. And lo and behold, there was a lone one-horned rhino in the distance emerging from the mist like a pre-historic animal. When the mist finally cleared, it laid bare a stunning tapestry of green grasslands dotted with blue waterbodies – the kind you see in the nearby Kaziranga and the faraway Dudhwa, both of which are the preferred habitats of the endangered one-horned rhino.

The jeep soon stopped at the forest quarters where our guide Sunil showed us the overnight pugmarks of a tiger, and the horn-marks of a rhino desperately needing mineral supplements.

We had an inquisitive co-traveller on our return. An owlet would fly ahead of us and patiently wait for us to catch up, and the moment we did, it would fly again to the next waiting branch. Almost as if inviting us to come and take a photograph which I eventually did. And then it disappeared.

Then there was the hog deer peering from behind a tree, a crested serpent eagle strategically perched on a tree top, a green pigeon that flashed past as a green streak, a rose-ringed parakeet that landed in slow motion next to its nest, and a warbler doing the balancing act on a moving blade of tall grass.

Back at the forest gate, as we were sipping black saay (that's how an Ahomi pronounces chaay), we saw a tame baby elephant Kaancha nibbling at the oltenga fruit, considered a delicacy by the elephants. And I thought to myself that good taste is inborn.

Nameri National Park

This park has a completely different topography from Orang and it adjoins the neighbouring state of Arunachal Pradesh.

A gentle walk of a kilometre from the Eco Camp takes you to the banks of the Jia Bhoroli river that is teeming with golden mahseer. And across the blue river you get the first panoramic view of this stunningly beautiful sanctuary.

A ride in a country boat takes you across to the forest department jetty, and then you walk on sparkling white pebbles scattered along the banks of the river like prehistoric eggs. The puddles on the riverbank have a reddish-brown algae that adds to the special aura of this landscape.

In the distance I saw a pair of ruddy shelducks, and the guide told us about a local myth. The fact that these ducks move around in pairs during the day and sleep separately in the night is interestingly explained in this story. It's believed that Lord Ram came to the neck of these forests looking for Sita when she was kidnapped by Ravan. And when he came across a lovey-dovey pair of shelducks, he asked them if they had seen Sita. The haughty male shelduck chided Ram, 'What kind of a husband are you that you can't even look after your wife?' Hearing this unjust insinuation, Ram turned as red as the ruddy shelducks and cursed them. 'Henceforth, you and your mate will only be together during the day. In the night you will be separated and you will spend the whole night pining for each other!' And the curse continues to be legally valid to this date.

The forest guard who doubled up as our guide proudly carried an antique single-barrel gun that hung from his shoulder on a frayed rope that was about to give way any moment. As he walked in front of me I kept stealing glances at the rope, wondering when it will break and the gun will come crashing down to the ground and go bang! Every guard in the forests of Assam has one such antique gun purportedly to be used against crouching tigers and hidden terrorists. But eventually it remains a mere psychological boost than a weapon of any potent use.

A few yards into the dense part of the forest, and there were tell-tale signs of a rampaging herd of elephants. The guide took a real close look at their dung, made a quick forensic analysis, and declared that it was around 48 hours ago that the elephants were here. Heaving a sigh of relief, we continued on our exploration. Only to run into a lone tusker fortunately separated from us by the security of a river in full spate. Further ahead was the clawmarks of a sloth bear on a tree trunk. Looking up we saw a bee-hive that must have drawn him here like a magnet.

Then we came across a patch of silk-cotton trees, leafless but with a flaming efflorescence covering the treetops. Flashes of colour were added to this arboreal flower garden: by green bee-eaters, scarlet minivets, emerald doves, red-whiskered bulbuls, golden orioles and purple sunbirds.

Ahead on an oltenga tree, I saw an animal seen only in the North-East: the Malayan squirrel. And this underlined the ecological fact that these beautiful forests in India were once contiguous with the verdant forests of Myanmar, Thailand, Malaysia and Indonesia.

Yes, much before the world became a global village, it was a global forest.

the painting is on the wall

It all started four decades ago: in the early 70s. Pupul Jayakar, the woman who unearthed many an Indian folk idiom, along with her assistant Bhaskar Kulkarni, was on a voyage of rediscovery. First they rediscovered the rich and colourful Madhubani art, and then the amazingly spartan idiom of Warli art that shunned the use of all colours except two: brown and white.

Jivya Soma Mashe, one of the accomplished Warli artists of the time, was invited to New Delhi for a demonstration of their art. In front of unbelieving eyes, on a sheet of brown paper Jivya drew the figure of Paalghaat, the Goddess of Fertility, sitting in the centre of an intricately drawn temple. When prodded to draw more visuals, Jivya drew a blank. He frankly admitted that this is all that every Warli artist knows to draw: the ritualistic drawing of the Goddess that is painted on the walls of a Warli house on the day of a wedding.

According to Phiroza Tafti, the convenor of the Dahanu Chapter of INTACH, Jivya was encouraged by Pupul Jayakar to break the shackles of convention and depict the rich mythology and the evocative legends of their tribe in their own inimitable Warli style. Jivya came back to his native village and had a meeting with other fellow artists. And once liberated from the strict traditions of ritualistic paintings, the floodgates opened and out flowed thousands of distinctly different Warli paintings: depicting their myths, folk tales and even their daily life. And Warli art moved from the depictions of God to the depictions of mere mortals.

On our visit to Dahanu in the northern belt of coastal Maharashtra, Phiroza Tafti offered to take us around the villages of the Warlis and share her experiences with us. All collected from the time she came to Dahanu as a newly-wed city-based rebel who made the chickoo orchard of her husband her permanent home.

A pilgrimage to the Waghoba Mandir was first on the list. Here we saw idols carved on totem poles. The totem pole was a relic from prehistoric times and the idol was a symbol of their unavoidable contact with the rest of the world. Originally the Warlis never worshipped man-made idols. The shaman of the village on his sojourn to the nearby hills would pick up small rocks that spoke with him in positive tones. These would then be kept under trees and they would become places of worship. Over many centuries, influenced by mainstream religions, the weather-beaten stones eventually took man-made shapes, and temples were built around them.

While inside the shrine of the Tiger God Waghoba, Phiroza insisted that we sit down and feel the vibrations of the place. And indeed as we closed our eyes in deep meditation, a certain calmness soothed our souls. Was it the sound of the stream that flowed nearby or was it the sound of the stream of consciousness?

The Warlis are a simple folk with simple beliefs that govern their simple lives. According to Yashodhara Dalmia, an authority on tribal arts and Indian anthropology, the Warlis are frugal in their habits and even in their speech.

A Warli woman, before she cooks supper, asks her family members how many 'bhakris' each one would eat that night. And she would then make exactly that number. When Yashodhara asked the woman why she does this every day, day after day, the woman replied, 'These bhakris are roasted on the back of Kansaari, the Goddess of Harvest. Why give her more pain than what's necessary?'

Another unique character of this tribe is that they speak very little, almost in monosyllables. That's because the Warlis believe words have an uncanny habit of suddenly becoming real. So they ensure they don't speak anything untoward lest it becomes true.

23

Probably in sheer contrast to this frugality, every Warli artist pours his heart out while painting. Though the figures are graphic, devoid of details and colour (like cave paintings), they are surprisingly rich in their choice of subjects: human figures in various situations, gods and goddesses, trees, plants, and animals. Even the minutest of them all, the ant, finds place in their paintings. As Yashodhara puts it so succinctly, 'The paintings are rich yet hieroglyphic in effect.'

Since Phiroza had to rush off to the school where she teaches, she assigned us to Yashode, her trusted Warli maid of 30 years. Yashode turned out to be more Warli than most: in terms of using words. While giving directions as I was driving, she would just point her hand to the left or the right without speaking a single word!

She took us to the house of Janu Ravte, a promising young Warli painter. First he took me to his studio, which he shares with six other artists of his cooperative. Then, after a cup of tea, he took us around his house that was barely lit by a skylight on the tiled roof, and a lone, small window. It was a wall such as this, smeared with mud and cow dung, that was the original canvas of Warli art. And staring at that dingy wall, I understood why the Warlis don't use colour but a white, rice-based paint to create their artworks. The sparkling white of the rice-paint gleams in the underlit house, catching even the faintest of sunrays that come in rather reluctantly. Giving the painting a truly ethereal feel.

Seeing Janu paint was a revelation. His hand was an extension of his mind, and his brush was an extension of his hand. It started with a basket and around it he weaved a tapestry of Warli life, all in a swirl of perpetual motion.

Today, in response to the thriving folk art market, villages after villages have taken up Warli painting; and in many cases the raw, creative energy has been replaced by static, decorative motifs that only have the purpose of being saleable. Underlining the fact that a painting becomes a work of art only if it's created by the forces inside, not the forces outside. And it's left to artists like Janu to uphold the fabulous traditions that have been transferred from one paint-brush to the next, across generations.

three shades of green

First I saw a real jungle marooned in a concrete jungle. Then a blue-green algae pond teeming with crocodiles. And then a blue lake with green reeds popping out like periscopes. Three shades of green with a hundred hues in between. All in a space of two days.

Guindy National Park

This National Park is situated bang in the middle of the bustling city of Chennai. A pair of green lungs surrounded by clogged arteries all around. The only other National Park in India that's located within city limits is Sanjay Gandhi National Park in Mumbai. But there's a vital difference between the two parks.

SGNP is a large tract of forest that's contiguous with an entire stretch that also lies outside the park. Namely, Tungareshwar Sanctuary and the forests of Thane district. This facilitates easy migration of wild animals which is crucial to the health of their species.

But here in Guindy, the tiniest National Park in India that admeasures just 270 hectares, the wild animals are cut off from the rest of their fraternity. So much so that the closest herd to the herd of blackbuck found here is all of 600 kms away in Point Calimere. Even spotted deer, jackals, pangolins and reptiles that exist here live in a marooned forest that floats in a concrete jungle. Thus encouraging inbreeding, which is not a healthy way to procreate.

Be that as it may, the 6 km walk along the periphery of the park was a delectable experience. On that path I came across the smell of rotten palm fruit that smelt exactly like toddy. A smell so inviting that toddy cats would have found it hard to resist it under the anonymous cover of night.

Then there was a slew of sights that would forever be recorded in my hard disk. Rhesus monkeys rappelling down an ancient rope into a deserted well and coming up as drenched beauties. A bouquet of butterflies sprouting on a wild plant. And a stag that had crashed through a wall of creepers and as a result had loose creepers dangling from its antlers, making it look like a real greenhorn.

Madras Croc Bank

In this park, apart from spotting the three species of crocodiles that are indigenous to India, I was keen to spot a member of another endangered species: Romulus Whitaker, a committed conservationist and the man who established this park. But I narrowly missed him as he had set off on a field visit to the Nicobar Islands that very morning.

The affable and knowledgeable guide Geetha made up for Rom's absence. She first introduced me to a crocodile that was the alpha male of the park, and was nicknamed Jaws. He was rescued as a baby and is the largest marsh crocodile ever to have been recorded in India. His feeding reminded me of the opening scene of Jurassic Park. The huge crocs in the nearby pond looked like lizards in comparison.

Pointing to a raised mound in the distance where the crocs lay their eggs, Geetha shared with me a very interesting biological fact about them. Their sex is not decided at the time of fertilisation but at the time of the hatching of the egg. If the egg is hatched when the outside temperature is below 31 degrees C, it becomes a female; and if the temperature is 31 degrees C or above, it becomes a male!

Geetha then took me to the stall of the Irula tribe as we were getting ready to leave. Here we met Maniyakaran, a tribal leader. He told me of the special relationship that Rom shared with the Irulas. On all his snake-watching expeditions, it was this snake-catching tribe that accompanied him sharing their deep knowledge of snake behaviour that they had gathered from pre-Dravidian times. These hunter-gatherers never took up farming but had perfected the art of finding grain to subsist. Rats steal grains from farms and hoard them in their holes. Snakes kill rats and start living there. Once the snakes vacate these places, the Irulas come in and raid the deserted pits. And easily pick up 8 to 10 kilos of grain from a single rat-hole. Who said you have to cultivate grains to reap a bumper harvest?

Pulicat Lake Bird Sanctuary

Pulicat is the second largest brackish lagoon in India after Chilika in Odisha. It has four islands bordering the Bay of Bengal. The biggest among them is Sriharikota, the island from which India's first lunar mission Chandrayaan was launched.

This lake interestingly has three rivers feeding it sweet water from one side, and the sea feeding it salt water from the other side. A dynamic and perennial exchange that breeds many species of vegetation, fish, waterbirds and reptiles that are unique to this ecosystem.

During the migratory season you see thousands of birds landing in the lake, as if it's raining feathers. Flamingos from Gujarat, painted storks from Siberia, and spoonbills from Eurasia. Many of them fall in love with this landscape and keep extending their visas, and eventually never go back to the land of their birth.

There's a beautiful road ringing this lake and sometimes even bisecting it. This road, along with the well-appointed benches and watchtowers that are strategically placed at regular intervals, give you a 180-degree ringside view of all the avian action.

The vast landscape reminds you of Kachchh, with endless stretches of land laden with salt and seashells.

Interestingly, Pulicat is the only bird sanctuary in India that straddles two states. In this case, Tamil Nadu and Andhra Pradesh. Bringing to the fore boundary issues among fishermen, and subsequent fishing in troubled waters. Apart from these local issues, a new ecological storm is brewing in the Bay of Bengal. Taking a cue from the historical fact this was a busy port in the 1st century, the powers-that-be in the 21st century are nurturing grandiose plans of converting this pristine sanctuary into a world class port and shipbuilding centre. Throwing to the wind environmental laws by blatantly reducing the Eco Sensitive Zone from 10 kms to a mere 2 kms.

As I sat on a lonely green bench and glanced at the horizon, I could see that the sun had decided to call it a day. Soon, sky colours began to mix magically with water colours, creating an enchanting landscape. And I hoped that the greed of man will not make this sun set on Pulicat Lake forever.

But don't take a chance. See it while it's still there. Offer open only till good sense lasts.

a birdsong for salim ali

There are two bird sanctuaries named after the father of ornithology in India, Dr. Salim Ali. One of them, Thattekkad in Kerala, teems with landbirds; while the other, Chorao in Goa, is rich in waterbirds. Thereby covering the entire wingspan of birdlife, and making it the perfect tribute to a man who celebrated birdwatching for close to 80 years.

Salim Ali was a legend in his own lifetime and a cartoon in the early 80s illustrated that. It showed a flock of Siberian cranes flying over Bharatpur sanctuary, with the leader of the group saying, 'Come, let's fly a little lower; if we are lucky we may be able to spot Salim Ali.'

Once, when he was all of 10, he wantonly shot down a sparrow in the jungles of Chembur, Mumbai. To his amazement he discovered that it had a yellow streak on its throat, just like a curry stain. He carried the bird home but even his uncle Amiruddin, the resident expert on birds, could not identify it. With a letter asking for help, Salim reached the office of the Bombay Natural History Society to meet the secretary, Walter Millard. The affable Walter instantly identified the bird as the yellowthroated sparrow, and then took young Salim to the cupboards of the bird museum where he opened drawer after drawer to show him a few hundred stuffed specimens of birds found in the Indian Subcontinent. And this sparked off a fire in Salim Ali that burned for over 80 years, and threw light on the lives and times of hundreds of birds in India. From the Himalayas to Arunachal Pradesh to Rajasthan to Kanyakumari.

With his poetic descriptions of birds he hooked many a bird lover. And I am only one of the legion of bird lovers he has fathered. The call of a Malabar whistling thrush would be described by him as the 'Whistling of an idle school boy who's happy to have bunked school'. The shy behaviour of the Malabar Trogon would be described as 'A bird so self-conscious of the bright colour on its front that when you go near, it would instantly turn away and show you its dull, boring back'. And instead of describing the call of the lapwing as 'ti-ti-tiwi,' he would say it has a call that sounds like 'Did-he-do-it'? These poetic expressions and light-heartedness are abundant in 'The Fall of a Sparrow,' a brilliant autobiography he wrote at the young age of 80.

His undiminished love of the winged wonders was evident till his death at the age of 91. When he was just 88, he travelled by a Naval ship to the Andamans (he had blanket permission to travel anywhere in India in any mode of transport, including those of the Armed Forces). And he disembarked on an uninhabited island, and stayed there alone watching birds for six days and six nights, till the Naval ship came back and took him back to the isle of his birth. It was not to write any paper on any species of bird at the dusk of his career, but simply because his soul was still yearning for birdsongs.

Thattekkad, Kerala.

In one of his sojourns to the south of India, Dr. Salim Ali discovered the bounty of birdlife in Thattekkad. At his behest it was declared a sanctuary in the year 1983. Later he was to accord the state itself the status of having the richest birdlife in the whole of India. The probable reason for this could be the absence of industrialization due to labour problems (a unique case of the reds helping the greens!), or because of the sheer diversity of Kerala's habitats: ocean, estuaries, backwaters, rivers, evergreen forests, deciduous forests, rolling grasslands, the works.

My first trip to Thattekkad was in the year 1992. Those days the road from Kothamangalam came to screeching halt at the Periyar river. And from there a boatman would row you across in a canoe that looked like it was hastily built.

Last year when I made my second trip I got an unpleasant shock when the car didn't come to a halt at the river, but instead sailed smoothly over a bridge. It was easier transport but the mysticism of being rowed across to your destination was gone forever.

Welcomed by a repertoire of birdsongs, we walked to a well-appointed office set in the middle of a dense forest formed between two of the tributaries of the Periyar river. Climbing two flights of wooden stairs we reached the tree house that was to be our home for the next few days. As I glanced through the window I saw a perfectly camouflaged flying lizard on a tree in the distance. And as if to welcome us, it came flying across and perched on the tree right next to the tree house.

We set out birdwatching in the late afternoon. There were 270 birds to spot in that birding paradise. We managed to spot around 75 in three hours. Some of them we saw; but most of them we only heard. That's when I remembered Dr. Salim Ali's dictum: 'Learn to identify a bird by its call. Because first you hear it and then you see it. And many a time you don't even get to see it.'

The next day was our tryst with the Ceylon frogmouth, an endangered bird that's endemic to the Western Ghats. No guide ever guarantees any sighting ever; but Maani assured us he would show us not just one, but three of these rare birds. He took us to a patch of forest where quite surprisingly all the plants had dried up leaves. Amidst them were three birds, so perfectly camouflaged that only Maani's eagle eye could have spotted them. Being nocturnal they couldn't see in broad daylight and they were staring at us without seeing us. It was a threesome: father, mother and baby. We clicked away to glory and got some pictures that were really up close and personal.

Chorao, Goa.

Floating in the backwaters of Mandovi and Mapusa rivers are four beautiful islands: Chorao, Divar, Jua and Cumbarjua. And situated in the mangroves of Chorao is probably the smallest bird sanctuary in India: Dr. Salim Ali Bird Sanctuary, measuring all of 2 square kilometres.

When we took the ferry from Ribandar, we could see the sanctuary across the river and it looked like any other mangrove forest. It was only after we landed there and walked along the one-kilometre pathway that we discovered it's truly a panoramic forest. At every turn the landscape was different; and there were as many as 14 different species of mangrove plants, submerged but surviving in the intricate maze of canals that run through the sanctuary. Some of these specially adapted plants were breathing with the help of roots that were jutting out from the tidal waters like periscopes.

The place abounds in resident wetland birds like plovers, herons, seagulls, sandpipers and kingfishers. And many migratory birds like pintail ducks and ruddy shelducks make this their winter home every year.

As you walk on the pathway beautifully laid out along the periphery of the mangroves, you witness a dual truth: on the left of the pathway along the backwaters is a long stretch of plastic garbage which is man's gift to Nature. And on the right are pristine mangroves in its greenest finery which is God's gift to mankind.

So when I saw a small bunch of school kids cleaning up the mess in the backwaters as part of their social work programme, I knew Dr. Salim Ali would be smiling behind his grey beard in quiet appreciation.

history, live!

History is brought alive in the most dramatic and spectacular ways in son-et-lumiere or sound-and-light shows. I had seen one in the imposing Red Fort, and one in the enchanting Golconda Fort. In these shows the ruins become a grand amphitheatre, and powerful narration accompanied by imaginative use of light and sound recreates the events of a bygone era. But it was only at the Cellular Jail in the Andamans that I realized that a son-et-lumiere show can be so intense that it can move you to tears. The baritone voice of Om Puri and the endearing voice of Naseerudin Shah recreated the mindless torture that was perpetrated on our freedom fighters in that bleak island called Kaala Paani. Torture so inhuman that it will put Guantanamo Bay to shame. I remember in tragic detail the story of Veer Savarkar. Made to live in a 5x5 cell for 11 solitary years, directly facing the place where they hanged a man almost every second day, the British tried to break his will. A diehard patriot that he was, he used to sing to the birds on the overhanging trees the patriotic poems that he had scribbled in the waking hours of the morning. And then he would ask them to learn these songs by heart and fly across the treacherous ocean and sing them freely in his motherland.

At the Residency in Lucknow, the theatre where India's First War of Independence was waged, sadly there was no sound-and-light show. But inspired by the awesome show in the Andamans, I created one in my mind, aided and abetted by the guide who narrated the story of the Lucknow Siege in historic detail.

During that war, which the British referred to dismissively as the Sepoy Mutiny, over 1300 Britishers living in the city of Lucknow panicked and took refuge in the residence of Sir Henry Lawrence. The advancing troop of freedom fighters trapped them inside the Residency in one of the bloodiest and longest sieges in the world. Supplies of food, water and medicines were completely cut off, and a fierce battle raged on. It took all of 27 days for a small relief platoon to break through the barricade, but soon they too were trapped inside. And the siege continued for another 60 gruelling days. Thousands died on either side; but it's believed that more captives died inside the Residency due to starvation and disease than due to bullets.

The remnants of the Residency today has a church, a mosque, a school, a post office, a jail and a stable. Each one deeply scarred with the pockmarks of cannon balls and sniper bullets. But the graveyard near the church shows the Great Imperial Divide. The Britishers have individual tombstones with flowery epitaphs engraved on them, whereas the Indians who fought for the British against their own brethren have been given an anonymous mass burial. Perhaps it was poetic justice for having betrayed their own brothers.

The red-brick structures stand in mute testimony to the will and the determination of the very first in our long line of freedom fighters. In those 87 days of embattlement the very edifice of the British Empire was shaken to its foundations; though it took another 90 years for it to completely come crumbling down.

It left me wondering why such a dramatic theatre like the Residency doesn't have a son-et-lumiere show. Probably it's because in India there is so much of history that every second stone we stumble upon is a relic. And familiarity breeds contempt of history.

borneo: as old as the hills

The oldest rainforests on this planet are not to be found along the banks of the Amazon in Brazil, but along the meandering rivers of Malaysia. They are home to more than 20% of the animal species in the world, many of them being endemic to these forests.

The flora too is extremely diverse; and it's believed that there are more plant species in one square mile of the rainforests here than in the whole of Europe put together. To give an idea of this diversity, in the mountain ranges of Kampung Bako alone there are over 400 varieties of palm.

We started our exploration of Borneo from Kuching, the capital of the Sarawak state. It was here in our hotel that we met Rives Puon, the finest forest guide I have come across in my three decades of travel. Born into the Bidayu tribe, he was educated in Kuching. He was extremely knowledgeable about the flora and fauna of the rainforests, and also about the various indigenous tribes of Sarawak. He spoke fluently, clearly, and had a tremendous sense of humour.

Semenggoh, the Orangutan Reserve

Three decades ago, a journalist named Ritchie rescued an orangutan held captive on the Indonesian border and brought him to the jungles of Semenggoh. Here he was nursed back to his wild ways and released into the forest. He was named Ritchie after his rescuer, and soon he inspired many such rescues. Today he is all of 40; and Semenggoh is a world-renowned rehabilitation centre where you can study the behaviour of the endangered orangutans in the wild. As the oldest member of the 27 orangutans living here, he is the master of all he surveys from the treetops, and is their alpha male.

My first glimpse of Ritchie was when he was swinging on the Tarzan vine like a consummate trapeze artiste, his orange fur lit up by the sunlight peeping through the morning mist. He then plunged headlong through the branches, bringing a huge branch down with him. And he walked towards us with the nonchalance of a king. He indeed had a tremendous presence: he was 5 feet tall, weighed 100 kilos, and had an arm span of 8 feet. The guides asked us to make way for the king, and warned us of his lethal 'love bite'. We all quickly moved aside, but not before I managed a shot of his captivating face, up close and personal.

Strictly speaking, these orangutans are semi-wild. Because, after their release into the wild they keep coming back to the centre for food. Initially, every day. Once they learn to gather food in the wild, infrequently. But during fruiting season, never. The second reason is that Semenggoh is a small patch of rainforest, measuring just 650 hectares and floating in a sea of human settlement merely 24 kms from the bustling city of Kuching. Cut off from any other rainforest, these primates are actually living in open captivity.

Orangutan in Malay means People of the Forest. The tribals here believe that once upon a time the orangutans lived with the humans. But being non-communicative and solitary in nature, they preferred to be left alone. And one day they eventually moved deep into the forest, thereby earning the sobriquet of People of the Forest. But the tribals never let them to go completely out of sight. Because it's the orangutans who teach them all about the ways of the forest, including telling them which fruits to eat and which ones to avoid.

Orangutans have a lifespan of around 50 years. But the tragic biological truth about them is that females can only give birth to one offspring, that too once in eight years. This low fertility, combined with the destruction of habitat, probably explains why they are critically endangered.

These primates are extremely territorial. And the reason is that each one needs a large tract of forest which has the choicest fruit trees in great abundance. But equally importantly it's also because they have the peculiar habit of moving house every day. So they abandon their nest-like resting place of the previous night, and painstakingly build a new 'nest' on a different tree. Every day.

On our return, we saw a cluster of pitcher plants. Slender and elegant, with a beautiful lid that's perennially open, it looks like anything but a carnivorous plant. The open pitcher emanates a smell that's a fatal attraction for insects. And once the unsuspecting insects (it's been happening for millennia; and at least by now they should have caught on) land on the slimy insides of the pitcher, they become totally immobile. The plant then closes the lid to make doubly sure there's no great escape. The insects are slowly dissolved by enzymes and sucked into the digestive tracts of the plant. Rives told us about a glorious exception: the 'Jain' pitcher plant! It too keeps the lid open; but when a few dew drops fall into it in the wee hours of the morning, it closes its lid in sheer bliss. And remains happy and content, drawing its nutrition from the dew.

Bako National Park

The oldest National Park in Malaysia is also one of South Asia's smallest. But amazingly in just 2700 hectares of forest it holds a very wide range of habitats. And you realize it the moment you reach Bako jetty. As you pan your eyes from one side to the other, you see beach vegetation, mangroves, marshes, grasslands, forests and even cliff vegetation. Each one holding in its bosom its own distinctive wildlife.

A 30-minute drive and a 30-minute boat-ride brought us here from the city of Kuching. En route we saw some awesome paintings created by Nature on volcanic rocks: in blue, brown, red, yellow, green and white (did I leave out any colour?). And a few sculptures floating in the ultramarine sea to match. It was God's own art gallery.

On our way to the guest house, we were welcomed by a strange-looking creature: a bearded pig loitering aimlessly on the beach. After freshening up, we headed to one of the 18 colour-coded trails that were drawn out by the forest department. The idea is to prevent the uninitiated from straying into the lurking dangers of the unknown. And right enough even my semi-trained eyes could not spot the venom of the perfectly camouflaged green pit viper that was just an arm's length away. Sometimes in Nature, it makes sense to walk the trodden path.

On one of the trees nearby we spotted the clown of the Malaysian forest: the proboscis monkey. With an oversized nose, it looked as if it had just walked out of a Pinocchio comic. Close by were silver leaf monkeys with their silvery fur glistening in the sun. Though both these monkeys are leaf-eating, they don't get into territorial fights. Simply because their choice of trees is completely different from each other. To each his own leaf.

Rives, a master in seeking out wildlife, spotted the elusive flying lemur on the tree top. It had its face turned towards the trunk, and it was after 15 minutes of patience that it turned and glanced at us for a few nanoseconds.

In the evening we walked along the mangroves. There, male fiddler crabs were flaunting their colourful and abnormally large claws to attract the females. But unfortunately some of them attracted the unwanted attention of crab-eating monkeys and ended up on their dining table.

Rives showed us a unique mangrove tree called sonarika that's a delicacy for the proboscis monkey. It has leaves so brittle that it crackles like potato chips when you break it; and the leaves are sweet on one side and salty on the other. Rives explained that the side that touches the seawater is salty, and as the water slowly passes through to the other side, it becomes sweet. It's literally a desalination 'plant'. Is there a technology here for humans to adopt? Nay, exploit?

It was becoming dark, and Rives knew exactly where the fireflies would be. Each species of fireflies has a different timing for flashing their torchlights. But sometimes females of a particular species imitate the timing of another species just to attract their males. And when these males do get attracted and land in the waiting arms of the femme fatale, they are killed and devoured.

And as the new moon started rising, Rives showed us the bread-fruit tree. On the third crescent of the new moon, tribals in Sarawak peel off the bark of this tree (when it's at its softest and most flexible) and make their costumes with it.

Another interesting flora we saw was a fern that had a symbiotic relationship with a frog. A group of this fern would grow in a circle forming a large bowl that would trap rainwater. The frog would lay its eggs here in thanksgiving, and in turn give the fern its nutrients in the form of droppings.

Gudung Gading National Park

Here's where you pray you find the largest flower in the world: the rafflesia. It's rare, endemic, and endangered. It takes all of nine months for the bud to blossom but the flower only lasts for seven days. And the flowering can occur anywhere in the 5,000 hectares of forest. At the park gate we were told that our prayers have been answered, and just the earlier day one had flowered very close to the jungle path. This flower is at its most colourful on the second day, after which it starts turning dark till it becomes as black as coal on the seventh day.

Rafflesia is a parasite with all its organs in a defunct state except for the flower. In fact all that you see with your naked eye is just a huge flower clinging on for dear life to its host liana or the Tarzan vine. The vine itself is an incredible specimen; and one single plant is recorded to have travelled as many as 5 kms in the rainforest here.

The flower is blood red in colour, and has the texture of flesh. And it also has the smell of rotten flesh to match. This is to attract the attention of the blow-ants that pollinate them. Despite these desperate measures pollination is rare, and that makes this plant endangered. The reason is that a male flower and a female flower have to blossom in close proximity for the tiny blow-ant to pollinate them in one go. And Nature being whimsical, such synchronization is few and far between. The rafflesia we saw was small: just two feet in diametre. Compared to the largest one recorded here that's close to four feet.

As a double delight we also saw the tallest flower in the world: the amorphophallus. It was about three feet in height, whereas the bigger ones among them are known to grow up to about eight feet.

At Gading I also met the exuberant Anthonia, a female forest guard. When she saw me clicking pictures, she took me to a tree to show me a lantern fly on one branch, and a flying lizard on another. She then showed me a few hundred amazing photos she herself had taken of the flora and fauna here. Ever since someone gifted her a camera five years ago, she has been documenting the life in these forests from dawn to dusk, round the year, year after year. That's when I realized the difference between being there for a day and being there every day. On most days, she goes into the forest at 5 in the morning and spends close to three hours in the lap of Nature. Anthonia was born in a village near the forest, grew up in the forest, and now works in the forest. Truly, a daughter of the forest.

a patchwork of green

For years, they dug into the bowels of a dense forest looking for stones. When quarrying hit the rock bottom in the early 70s, it was banned. But by then the destruction of this beautiful forest called Manpada was near complete.

When the extent of the tragedy dawned on the forest department, they went on a green frenzy. And instead of planting the indigenous trees that were destroyed, imported trees were randomly planted. The simplistic logic was: 'A tree is a tree is a tree'. So acacia and gliricidia from Australia, English tamarind from the United States, and gulmohar (yes, this beautiful tree with a beautiful Indian name is actually an import) from Madagascar were planted arbitrarily across the forest.

The problem with these trees was that they guzzled too much water, thereby reducing the ground water level. And the other problem was that they also spread uncontrollably. Along with these foreigners, came certain weeds that too spread like green cancer. Candy floss, Mexican poppy and lantana: each one of which systematically wiped out the local plants. In fact, lantana is a great threat to local vegetation because of its strange habit of secreting toxic chemicals from the roots that destroy any sapling that tries to grow near it.

Soon the colonialisation of the forest was complete. When local conservationists protested, a few saplings of subabool, bamboo, Indian rosewood, bauhinia, khair and an interesting tree called monkey biscuit tree were planted in small numbers. (The latter is called so because monkeys relish its seeds that are shaped like biscuits.) And slowly the Indian trees started taking on the might of the foreigners.

Hearing these forest tales from Kaustubh Bhagat of BNHS, we started our trek from the eastern gate of Sanjay Gandhi National Park where Manpada is located. It is a part of the Yeoor Range in Thane, and adjoins the beautiful open-air butterfly park called Ovalekarwadi.

The first sighting was the Quarry Lake. It was a lake formed in the bowel of a large deserted quarry. But it looked beautiful with egrets, kingfishers and herons waiting at the water's edge for their catch of the day. It was like a blue balm applied on a brown wound.

Then we witnessed three types of predatory hunting. Very close to the lake was a khair tree and we spotted a shikra lying in wait for its prey. Unlike the big raptors like kites and eagles, they are small in build with smaller wings. So they don't swoop down from the skies on spotting a prey. They wait, perched on the lower branches of a tree, and pounce on an unsuspecting prey from close quarters.

The strategy of the palm swifts was very unique. They flew about in the sky in unpredictable paths, holding their mouths wide open. And their prey, which are essentially small insects, would simply enter their gaping mouths and get stuck on their slimy sides.

On the other hand, the bee-eaters would sit facing the sun, and once the wings of their prey got lit up by the sun, they would chase them and catch them acrobatically in mid air. A bee-eater flew alongside as we trekked, and demonstrated in front of us her mastery in aerial combat.

Different wings, different strategies. Mother Nature has worked it all out in the minutest detail.

Soon we came across a patch of bamboo grove. The interesting thing about bamboo is that they live up to sixty years; and then they all flower and die. In this patch, all the bamboos had died of old age, all at once, and tiny saplings were slowly taking their place in the forest sun.

The forest floor was teeming with life. As Dr. Rahmani of BNHS says, that is where you will find myriads of life forms. And looking for bigger wildlife, we end up missing the floor for the forest. Right in front of us was a butterfly called peacock pansy. This beautiful creature had four eyes on its wings to make it look so diabolic that predators are warded off.

There was a slender snake slithering into the dry leaves. It was called the slender coral snake, and had a distinct black head. A peculiarity about this snake is that, though extremely poisonous, it has a mouth that opens just a wee bit. So it can't bite off more than it can chew. Such is the profound balance of Nature.

Looking back at the forest, I realized that it looks more like a garden and less like a forest because of the dominance of imported flowering trees. And I realized that once a forest is destroyed, it is impossible to bring it back to its original glory. Because you can only plant trees, you can't plant the intricately balanced forest floor with its myriad life forms that has taken so many millennia to evolve. And all attempts at afforestation merely become a patchwork done on a tapestry that's lost forever.

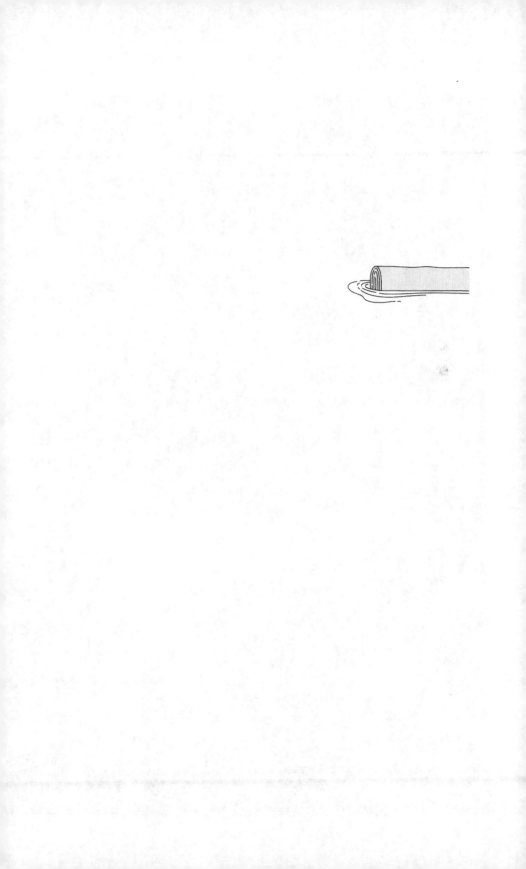

the unknown backwaters

There's a poem in Malayalam that describes the serene beauty of Kerala. It roughly translates as: 'She has her head resting on the lush green pillows of the Sahyadris and her feet dangling in the deep blue waters of the Arabian Sea; and her immaculate body is adorned with the ornaments of the backwaters.'

These ornaments crisscross the entire stretch of the state from Thiruvananthapuram to Kasargod, and measures over 900 kilometres in its undulating length. It is a blue-green labyrinth made of canals, lakes and rivers. The most picturesque of them is in the southern part of Kerala and spreads over four districts: Ernakulam, Alappuzha, Kottayam and Kollam. It comprises five large lakes interlinked by canals, and breastfed by 38 rivers.

Says Manu Menon, a naturalist and wildlife photographer based in Kerala, 'Due to the dynamic nature of these waterbodies where sea water and sweet water continuously intermingle with each other, a unique ecosystem is created. Here a wide spectrum of flora and fauna, of both the sea and the sweet water variety, have been living in perfect harmony for millennia'.

Adjoining these backwaters is another habitat called Kol wetlands that's unique to Kerala. The major ones being in Parappur, Vembanad and Ashtamudi. Much like it happens in Kachchh in Gujarat, large swathes of land near the backwaters get completely submerged in water during the monsoon creating innumerable islands. When the water drains off from here after the rains, they once again become flatlands where paddy is cultivated from October to March. As many as four species of migratory fish have been recorded in the Kol wetlands, and they have been declared as a Ramsar site for their international ecological significance.

Just as there are National Highways in the rest of India, there are National Waterways in Kerala. The longest of them is National Waterway No.3 that runs from Kollam to Kottappuram for a marathon distance of 205 kms.

I had done the highway four years ago. We had stayed on a kettuvallam or a houseboat for a night and two days at the ever-popular Kumarakom. I still remember sleeping on the deck under a canopy of twinkling stars. Much before that I had spent a night at deep sea, near Bhayander in Mumbai. And the difference between the two nights was dramatic. Though it's the same canopy of stars that you sleep under in the deep sea, the wobbly fishing boat makes you feel insecure, and with no land in sight anywhere you feel like a lonely speck in the infinite universe. But in a houseboat in the backwaters, you are the centre of the universe, safely cocooned in the orchards of swaying coconut palms.

This time I decided to stay away from the National Waterways and take a small bylane instead. My search for uncharted waters took me to the backwaters of Murinjapuzha, which literally means the Sliced River. A tributary of Moovattupuzha, it is 25 kms long as the duck swims.

At the 'tea shaap,' as I was sipping tea and nibbling at a parippu vada (or dal vada for the uninitiated), the President of the local Panchayat told me, 'Saar, what you have done is right. It is high time tourists leave Kumarakom and Alappuzha, and explore these virgin waterways instead.' And true to his words, in the amazing waterways of Murinjapuzha there were no traffic jams of houseboats. The channel was being criss-crossed only by small country boats and smaller canoes.

This island is just one of the hundred islands that dot these untested backwaters spread over 20 square kilometres. The smallest of them is just a few acres and uninhabited; and the largest is around 3 square kilometres with over 1700 houses, churches, temples, schools and hospitals.

It's a world interconnected only with waterways, and a boat is the only mode of transport. So you go to school by boat, you go to work by boat, you go to the market by boat, and of course you visit your neighbour's house by boat. So each house has a parking lot for the boats, and everyone in the house - men, women and children - are adept at rowing to their destination.

Anju Jose was the man who introduced me to this amazing waterworld. Unlike the huge, luxurious kettuvallams or houseboats that can be moored only in deep water, and are therefore kept at a respectable distance from the shores, Anju's boat could approach the land at will. Whenever the water became shallow, he would quietly dismantle the motor and fish out the huge bamboo pole for rowing closer to the land.

Thus we touched base at many places in the three large islands of Poothotta, Chempu and Murinjapuzha, and many more tiny ones.

In all the smaller islands, there was a peculiar problem: 'Water, water, everywhere; not a drop to drink.' Though surrounded by an abundant quantity of brackish water, there are no sweet-water sources on these islands. So the water available on the islands is used only for bathing, washing vessels and washing clothes. And in one of these islands, I saw the paradoxical sight of water being transported on water.

There was a whole new world out there waiting to be explored. And standing on the hull of the boat, I felt the same thrill as Ibn Batuta the Moroccan traveller, and Marco Polo the legendary explorer, both of whom had been here many centuries ago. First there was the Magic Island, which even the smallest canoe could not approach as the water was only one foot deep all around for a radius of half a kilometre. So you had to wade through knee-deep water for 25 minutes to reach there. Then there was this necklace of islands each of which had its chosen occupation. So there were islands that had poultry farms, duck farms, banana plantations, prawn farms, Chinese fishing nets, toddy-tapping, sand-dredging, shell-meat collection, lime production, coir-making etc.

I met an old lady on Chempu island who was weaving magic. Using a small wooden contraption, she was getting unruly strands of coconut fibre to form a small rope, and was then getting two such small ropes to merge into one just like two entwined serpents.

As our country boat took a U-turn on the waterway, I saw the high tide coming in. And I fervently hoped that it only was the usual high tide, and not the rising sea water caused by global warming as recently reported in the newspapers. When that eventual deluge happens, many of these tiny islands will face a watery death and the beautiful waterscapes of Kerala would then change forever. See them while they are still there.

where past is present

Lucknow is a city that's enveloped in itself. A 400-year-old tradition of style and panache is frozen on the walls of its monuments, but it is still flowing in the hearts of its wonderful people.

When the Mughals lost control of this region, the Nawabs of Avadh took over. Patrons of all forms of art, they were particularly generous when it came to architecture, dance, music and the culinary arts. There's a curious story regarding the last of these arts. It's said that one of the last nawabs was extremely fond of kababs. He would have them for breakfast, lunch and dinner. But as he aged, he lost his teeth and couldn't undertake the rigours of chewing. Feeling bad for the old man, the master chef Haji Murad Ali invented a master recipe of a kabab that doesn't have to be chewed; it merely melts in your mouth. It's called Tunday Kebab and is served even today at a traditional restaurant called Tunday Kababi run by the descendants of Murad Ali on Aminabad Road.

The unique sights and smells of Lucknow can best be experienced on this road. Here you will find crowds milling about, and cycle rickshaws deftly slicing them into two without spilling a single drop of blood. Here you will find no general store. Everyone is a specialist. So you have shops that sell only attars, only pickles, only silverware, only chikan work, only zaris, only masalas, or only flowers.

It was outside my hotel that I met a man who stood for all that Lucknow stands for. He was wearing a shirt that had weathered many a summer; yet he had a royal demeanor. He welcomed me with a disarming smile and said, 'Aadab!' I returned the greeting and was about to walk away when he asked me if he could take me somewhere. I replied that I don't go by cycle rickshaws as I felt it is a cruel way of transportation. He calmly told me, 'Just change the way you look at it. Don't see me as an animal pulling a man, but as a man carrying another man on his shoulders in the time of need.' Looking into the dire need in his eyes, I relented.

For the next two days, he was my charioteer. He decided the places I should see, and he decided my itinerary. The more I saw of him, the more he reminded me of Balraj Sahni, the legendary Indian actor.

Bada Imambara was the grandest of them all. Built by Nawab Asaf-ud-daula in 1784 to provide relief to his subjects during a calamitous famine, it's a true architectural wonder. Colossal in size, it has a large central hall that is 170 feet long and 50 feet high. The beauty of the construction is that there is not a single pillar supporting this structure and marring the view of this grand spectacle. My charioteer-cum-guide told me the secret of how this structure was made cyclone-proof. Bada Imambara has a network of labyrinths called 'bhoolbhulaiyas'. These are built all along the periphery of the structure. When you enter one such passage, it takes you to four passages: one of them is right, the other three are dead-ends. And every right passage takes you to four more, and so on. Chances of finding the right way here are as high as the sun rising in the west. Open to the outside world through small windows, these passages are actually 'air passages' that disperse the cyclonic winds when they hit the structure.

Chhota Imambara is more ornate in design. And replete with coloured chandeliers, gilt-edged mirrors and the royal throne of the Nawab. But sadly a misplaced coat of paint had been applied to this structure that had aged so gracefully with time. In the compound you will also find the replica of the Taj Mahal, and an immaculate structure with black and white calligraphy.

The other wayside beauty as Satkhanda, a perennial work in progress. Originally conceived as a 7-storeyed watchtower, the work was stopped half way after four storeys were constructed. Next to it is a red-brick structure that epitomizes the beauty of British architecture: the Husainabad Clock Tower that stands 220 feet tall, and is said to be larger than the famed Westminster Clock Tower.

The Char Baug, along with the Railway Station in Jodhpur and our own Chhatrapati Shivaji Terminus in Mumbai, stands among the most beautiful of all railway stations in India. And the Council Hall among the finest government offices anywhere in the world.

The fact that Lucknow is cut off from the rest of the world is so beautifully illustrated in a short story by Premchand. It's a story about the last Nawab of Avadh, Wajid Ali Shah, playing a battle of chess with his friend when the British were engaged in a battle with his army for taking over Lucknow. While Wajid Ali concentrated on winning on the chess board, his kingdom was taken over by the British and he was summarily exiled to Kolkata. Such were the vagaries of Indian rulers.

After my supper on Aminabad Road I left for my hotel room. And in a matter of seconds a man started running through the overcrowded lanes, brushing aside people and cycle rickshaws, looking for a bearded man with long white hair. When he did find me, he handed over my cellphone that I had forgotten on the restaurant table, and said 'Khuda haafiz'. And with deep gratitude in my heart, I said 'Shukriya'.

And from that moment till I left Lucknow two days later I kept looking for two faces in the crowd: my own Balraj Sahni and the man who returned my mobile. I didn't find them; and I'm sure I won't find them again on Facebook or Twitter or LinkedIn. But they will stay with me forever, in the recesses of my heart.

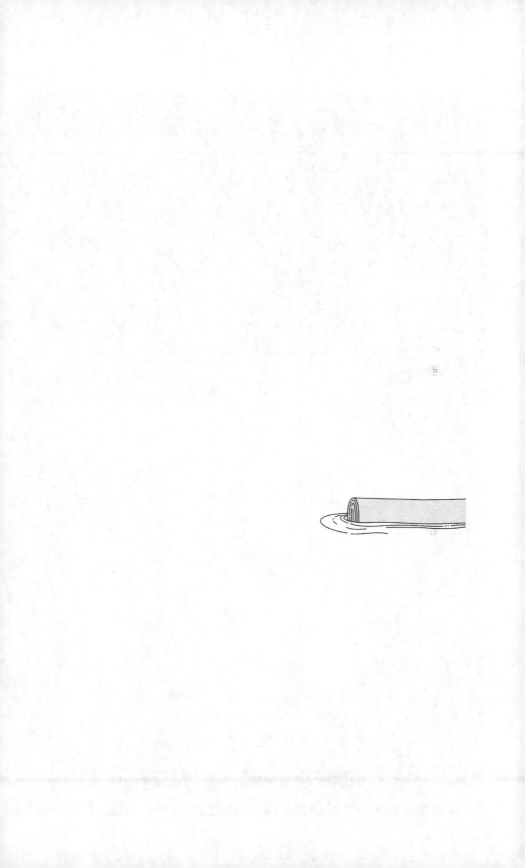

the last piece of a jigsaw

In the year 2010, Chandoli National Park was declared as part of the Sahyadri Tiger Reserve. Thus the missing piece of a green jigsaw fell in place, making a large tract of the forests in the Western Ghats in Maharashtra into one contiguous stretch.

Chandoli on one side adjoins the Koyna Sanctuary, and on the other, the Radhanagari Sanctuary. Providing a corridor for tigers and leopards to reach the forests of Goa, just in case they choose to take a long walk.

The drive to Janabai's mango tree was an exercise in mud-track rally driving. The looming mango tree was at least a 100 years old and had a story behind it. Janabai, a generous woman of her times, had given money to the shepherd community here called the dhangars. Thus helping them pay the land tax to the British during pre-independence days. In her honour they planted a mango sapling, and today it towers over 200 feet and is seen with its head and shoulders above the other forest trees, from as far away as 5 kms.

Back at the base, we attended a training programme conducted under the watchful eyes of one of the finest forest officers I have had the fortune of meeting: Mohan Karnat, Chief Conservator of Forests, Kolhapur. A team of about 80 guards and officers were imbibing the latest methods of GPS tracking using state-of-the-art wireless systems, setting up of camera traps, and familiarization with the new laws that have just empowered them.

A birding trip was on the cards the following morning. The excitement was palpable as we came across the massive hoof-marks of a herd of bison as they cascaded down a hill slope. In another patch, wild boar had uprooted edible plants for dinner last night. Then there were tree pies, babblers, paradise flycatchers, woodpeckers, drongos and scarlet minivets giving us company.

When we returned, Mohan told me with paternal glee in his eyes that three tiger cubs have just been sighted in the Reserve. But the location was not disclosed as it's a closely guarded secret known to just a couple of trusted officers. He then introduced us to an amazing plant expert, Shrirang Shinde, a forest guard based at Koyna.

Shrirang accompanied us all the way from Chandoli to Satara where I was to drop him. Right through our journey, which turned out to be a real botanical expedition, he opened out his green book, a leaf at a time.

Even as I was driving at 60 kmph, he would spot a plant whizzing past and would ask me to stop. He gave up studies after class 10 as his parents could not afford his further studies. And he considers himself fortunate to have he met his guru Dr. Sanjay Limaye, who opened up a whole new green world for him. Together they traversed the length and breadth of the Sahyadris on foot, discovering the secret lives of local plants. Unfortunately Shrirang lost his guru to the dreaded tsunami of 2004 in the Andaman and Nicobar islands.

Soon after we left Chandoli, he made us stop near a waterbody. Here I witnessed one of the most innovative uses of two different devices. Since he had a small camera with no zoom lens, he would hold his magnifying glass close to the plant and would photograph it through the glass to get a magnified image.

Near Karad, on a stopover to see a plant, he realized he could not identify it. So he took a picture of it to show it to his octogenarian mother who was his go-to authority, extremely knowledgeable about the plants in that area.

Shrirang then showed us a whole lot of incredible plants: Bamburti, a plant that is used by locals to preserve dead bodies. Daatpadi that is fed to cattle to increase their weight just before a village auction. Chirkha which on being fed to a dying cow will make the cow stand up, albeit for a few minutes. Agara the grain that is used by locals as food during drought, as it is the only plant that survives in parched conditions.

At Kaas I was fortunate to witness a beautiful sight. Shrirang Shinde, who has been studying the flora of the Western Ghats for almost three decades, was part of a team that discovered a new species of grass. It was named Eulalia shrirangi after the master botanist Shrirang Yadav. But as Shrirang Shinde was his namesake, I saw the unforgettable image of Shrirang holding a shrirangi in his hand.

the welcome shores

By the end of the 7th century, the mighty Sassanian Empire had been vanquished by Arab invaders. Many people of the Zoroastrian faith were consequently killed. Those who survived fled to the mountains of Iran. They were hounded out from there too, and after a brief respite in the town of Hormuz they set sail for India.

The ship that carried them was soon enveloped in a massive storm. The ship was rocked but not their faith. They prayed till the storm passed. And suddenly they discovered that they were washed ashore on the welcome shores of Nargol in Gujarat.

Legend has it that their leader, a Dastur, led his people to the durbar of the king of Sanjan named Jadhav Rana. When the Dastur requested permission for his people to settle down in Sanjan, the king asked for an empty vessel and some milk. Then, in full view of all those present, poured the milk into the vessel till it was full to the brim. And gave it to the Dastur, as if to mean there is no place in the kingdom to accommodate his people. The Dastur in turn took the vessel of milk in his hand, sprinkled sugar into it, gave it back to the king, and smiled. The vessel didn't spill over but had become sweeter. The king was so impressed with this brilliant metaphor that he gave them permission to settle down in Sanjan. And thus began one of the greatest integrations of two communities ever witnessed in the world.

At Nargol, where the Parsis first landed, I found a cluster of white-washed walls enclosing beautiful heritage houses, mostly manned by caretakers. After a lazy walk along its sleepy lanes, I found four kilometres of virgin beach with endless casuarinas whispering the tales of a bygone era. And as I left my footprints on the white sands, I realized this beach is almost unaware of its own existence.

A few years after settling down in Sanjan, the Parsis requested the king to allow them to build a Fire Temple. The Sacred Fire, according to their religion, is the Son of Ahura Mazda, or the Eternal Light. And this Fire is made out of 16 fires. 15 of them come from earthly sources like a brickmaker's kiln, a goldsmith's fire, a baker's oven, a shepherd's house, a crematorium, a king's house etc. The 16th fire is from a fire caused by lightning that comes from the heavens. The consecrated fire then occupies pride of place in the sanctum sanctorum of a Fire Temple. It took three years to purify this fire, and after it was placed in the Sanjan temple it burned bright for 669 years till the Mughals under Sultan Mahmud attacked Sanjan in the 13th century. The Parsis who had laid down their arms picked them up again. And 1400 valiant warriors under Ardeshir fought alongside the king's army. The Mughals defeated them after a bitter battle. Fearing the kind of persecution which their forefathers had suffered at Arab hands, the Parsis fled to the mountains of Bahrot, 20 kms away. With the most valuable possession of them all: the Sacred Fire.

The journey of the Sacred Fire shows the supreme will power and the sagacious nature of this community. It was hidden in the caves of Bahrot for 12 years, then taken to the jungles of Vansda for 14 years, then it remained safe in Navsari for 313 years, 3 years in Surat, back in Navsari for 5 years, then in Valsad for 1 year, till it reached Udvada in 1742. This sublime fire has been burning bright for 270 years now at the Fire Temple of Iranshah Atash Behram here.

Though they number just 60,000 in a population of 1.2 billion, some of the finest Indians have come from this miniscule community: lawyers and jurists, doctors, army officers, writers, dancers, artists, industrialists, to name a few. Philanthropy runs in their veins and the greatest charitable trusts are run by them. They not only take care of their elderly, but have built their Old Homes in the finest of locations in and around Mumbai, and in the hill stations of Matheran, Lonavla and Mahabaleshwar. And of all the communities living in India, they have the deepest concern for preserving nature and wildlife. With the possible exception of the Bishnois of Rajasthan.

At Sanjan, there is no trace of the original Fire Temple, nor are there any quaint Parsi houses. There is only a commemorative pillar that was built a century ago to mark the place of arrival of the Parsis in India.

Drive along the sea from Udvada and you will reach the twin beaches of Bordi and Gholvad. Known as the chikoo bowl of Maharashtra, they offer some fine Parsi cuisine too. Gool Khush is the pick of the Parsi restaurants offering you the best of class. Walk as much as you can on the deserted beach that stretches all of 17 kms, yes 17 kms. And once you have worked up a large appetite, feast on lagan-nu-bhonu, sali boti, mutton dhansak, kheema-pao, dal-pulao, patra-ni-machchhi, and top it up with caramel custard. Or if you prefer, walk along the patchwork of light and shade in a shaded chikoo orchard nearby, and take a deep breath. The aroma of toffee you get comes from the resin of the chikoo trees, and can serve as an alternative dessert.

Close by is the picturesque Asavali Dam, built painstakingly by hand, stone upon stone, much like how the pyramids were made. The dam has a mosaic of paddy fields on one side and tranquil blue waters on the other side encircling the hills in the distance. Up among those hills are the Bahrot Caves where the Parsis kept their holy fire safe and burning for 12 long years.

Yes, the Parsis have survived against all odds and have done wonderfully well in the land that adopted them. They have indeed been the sugar that for centuries has sweetened the flavour of the Indian ethos.

It is believed that Prophet Zarathustra, unlike other mortal kids, laughed when he was born. Probably, looking at the way the Parsis have integrated so well into this country, he would be smiling now.

rainspotting

In a land where it rains for 9 months in a year, even rain becomes drenched in mythology. It is believed in Kerala that at the height of summer massive birds called hornbills collect on bare treetops. They open their gigantic beaks and look longingly into the heavens praying for rains. When the intensity of their prayer becomes unbearable to the heavens, they open up. Quenching the thirst of these birds, and of every living being in Kerala.

In the oppressive heat of Malshej, I looked around for these hornbills on bare treetops. I couldn't spot them. Somewhere unseen and unheard, in the deep innards of the forest, they must have been perched on lifeless trees praying for rains.

All the trees on the mountain slopes were denuded and formed a wide sea of brown. The only exceptions were the laburnum and mayflower trees. Molten sunlight had collected on the branches of laburnum as golden yellow flowers. And the searing heat of May had coagulated as blood-red flowers on the mayflower trees.

As I gazed at the bare mountain ranges in front of me, I realized that every season, including the unforgiving summer, has its own charm. Since the mountains were shorn off the last tinge of green by the scorching sun, the rock faces had become nude. And I could feast my eyes on the delicate curves and contours of the mountains. Once the rains come pouring down, layers and layers of clothes would be draped on these mountains. And then you would have to wait till the next summer to appreciate their vital statistics.

The drive from Mumbai takes you to Kalyan, and a little beyond is a village called Tokavade. From here a series of wildly beautiful mountain ranges start unfolding in front of your ever-widening eyes. And this spectacle goes on for all of 90 kms. Yes, you read it right, 90 kms.

As the road first winds through the plains and then through the mountains, you see the most mystical and magical vistas of the entire Western Ghats. But sadly it's a spectacle you can never capture in your camera. Simply because it gradually unfolds all around you in 360 degrees, like a 'surround' spectacle. The entire mountainscape changes at every turn, and at every corner there's a picture postcard waiting for you. Each changing angle giving you a different shape of the same mountain, in a totally different light. Since shooting was not an option, I decided to do something even better. I clicked them in my mind and stored them in the infinite hard disk of my mind, with a special instruction not to delete them till my last breath.

The climax of this visual drama is staged when the mountain suddenly plateaus at Malshej. As you drive through a roughly-hewn tunnel, you are face to face with the sheer magnificence of towering peaks and bottomless valleys. And standing at land's very end, you gaze at what can only be described as the Grand Canyon of India, with the main difference being the faded green that's brushed onto the brown mountain slopes. If you happen to scream in sheer joy, your voice echoes back as if in affirmation.

At Malshej the long bund of Pimpalgaon Joga holds back the waters of Pushpavati river, creating a blue-green lake that swells in monsoon. If you walk along this bund in August, you may see pink clouds descending into the lake in the distance. And that's a sure sign of your tryst with flamingos at the next turn of the lake.

With Malshej as your base, you can drive down to Shivneri fort, 25 kms away. It was at Shivneri that the great Maratha king Shivaji was born. In a distinguished military career spanning decades, Shivaji had only one regret. Despite building and conquering over 250 forts in his lifetime, he could never conquer the fort of his birth. Paradoxically it took two generations; and his grandson eventually captured it in the 18th century. Such are the quirks of history.

As I drove back from Lenyadri to Malshej, the scorching heat played tricks on my mind. In the mirage created on the mountain road ahead, I could see rain falling upwards and waterfalls rising into the skies instead of falling into the valley. And I thought to myself that these are just my projections into the near future. Come July, these would happen in real, when massive eddie currents would sweep the entire Malshej landscape, and you would be able to witness the unbelievable sight of water at the edge of the cliff defying Newton's Law of Gravity.

Yes, Malshej is waiting for the magical rains. And for responsible travellers who would come to Malshej and leave it like they found it. Pure and pristine.

ripples in the sand

The Manganiyars have created ripples in the endless sand dunes of Rajasthan with their soulful singing.

I first met them 20 years ago in Shilpagram in Udaipur. They were regaling audiences in this unique miniature India, replete with rustic houses from every state, designed by the master artist Haku Shah. As they sang songs that were a heady blend of classical and folk, they got into a Sufi-like trance, celebrating the joy of living in the moment, and getting lost in it.

My journey to the land of their birth took me to a quaint village named Kanoi that sleeps in the sand dunes of the Thar desert, near Jaisalmer. Walking the bylanes here, I discovered that there are no farmers here and no herdsmen. Music is their living, and every house has a musician. And even the walls of their humble houses have ears. For music.

Though most of the singers in this village were on musical tours across the world, I was fortunate enough to meet Ishaq Khan, the only singer who had stayed back for some personal reasons. He assembled the khadtaal and the khamaicha players in no time, and put up a private performance on the verandah of his house. There was just my wife and me in the audience, apart from a bunch of kids who were unknowingly imbibing the early lessons of a rich oral tradition that has been passed on from generation to generation.

From Kanoi, I went to another Manganiyar village named Khuri about 60 kms away. Here I met a septuagenarian singer, Jalal Khan, who shared with me the reasons why their community is unique. Though they are born Muslims, they sing praises of Allah and many Hindu gods with equal gusto. Interestingly, every performance of theirs starts with an invocation of Lord Krishna. Small wonder, because every Manganiyar is a Sufi at heart.

As I was sitting on Jalal Khan's cot sipping tea laced with the salty taste of camel milk, he shared with me another peculiar tradition of the Manganiyars.

Here, children are only given temporary nicknames. Once the community recognizes them as great singers or musicians, each of these kids is allowed to choose a name of their liking. And they will be then known to the world by that name. Talk about earning a name for oneself.

But then Jalal pointed out an anomaly. One of the most well-known singers among them is called Kachra which means garbage. How come he chose such a self-effacing name for himself? Therein hangs a tale. And Jalal shared it with me. For many years, Kachra Khan's parents were childless. When they heard about a Sufi saint who had come a-visiting their village, they went to see him. And told him, 'We have been childless for many years. Please bless us with a child.' The Sufi saint told them that they will soon have not one but two children. Provided they agree to his condition. He said, 'Your first child will be born a good singer. When the time comes, let him choose his name. But your second son will be born a genius. You should name him Kachra.' The bewildered couple agreed but wanted to know the reason behind this strange command. The saint clarified, 'Though he will be born a genius, and will get fame at a very young age, success would go to his head and cause his downfall. The name Kachra will help him stay firmly rooted to the ground, all through his life.'

In the simmering sand dunes behind Jalal's house, I saw the reason why the Sufi saint said that fame and fortune are just mirages. You think they are real, but they don't exist.

the deserted beauty

The inhabitants of most historical monuments you see today, be it a palace or a fort, have been forcibly evacuated from there by the invaders.

Kuldhara in Rajasthan is probably the only place in the world where an entire population of over 17,000 people vacated en masse, of their own accord, and disappeared into the thick of a mysterious night.

It was with a great sense of excitement that I visited the twin-villages of Kuldhara and Khaba, 30 kms to the west of Jaisalmer in Rajasthan. These two villages, along with 82 other villages, were deserted overnight by the Paliwal Brahmins who lived here for over 5 centuries: from 1291 AD to 1825 AD.

As a Rajasthani folk song about this mass migration goes, 'Let's leave the calves in the stables, let's leave the cradles, let's leave the milk boiling on the cooking fire; let's leave all that we have here, never to come back again.'

The Paliwals were astute businessmen who controlled the trade on the Silk Route to Iran and the Arab lands. They were also visionary farmers who knew a lot about water conservation and rain harvesting, and miraculously cultivated wheat and gram in these harsh deserts. Then what made them make the supreme sacrifice of deserting their homeland, leaving behind the colossal wealth they had created over five centuries?

Stories abound. One says that Salum Singh, the prime minister of the King of Jaisalmer, was so envious of the prosperity of the Paliwals that he levied taxes so atrocious that they became the last straw on the camel's back.

Another one says that Paliwal women were stunningly beautiful, but the beauty of the Chieftain's daughter had to be seen to be believed. And the Rajput King of Jaisalmer was so smitten by her that he had decided to kidnap her and forcibly marry her. Be that as it may, the heads of all the 84 villages decided to leave their homes overnight, never to return. But before they left they buried their treasures, giving a damning curse that those who make an attempt to settle down in these villages will drop down dead.

And the third story goes that once in a while, skeletons of human bodies are found in the by-lanes of this ghostly village.

On my way out, I saw the Cactus Park near the main gate of Kuldhara village. And I wondered. Is the cactus symbolic of the survival spirit of the Paliwals who thrived in the harshest of conditions? Or is the thorn on the cactus symbolic of the harsh treatment meted out to them by the rulers of Jaisalmer? Maybe for all you know, it's both.

the temple town sanctuary

If you have saved up your holidays for a rainy day, and are planning to spend a few days on the lofty mountain peaks of Maharashtra where clouds don't rain but gently sprinkle water, I have a suggestion. Skip the oft-visited hill stations of Matheran and Mahabaleshwar and head straight to Bhimashankar, situated at an enthralling height of over 3700 feet. Here you will get the best of three worlds: a hill station, a wildlife sanctuary, and a 300-year old temple – all rolled into a neat, green bundle.

Legend has it that a demon called Tripurasura was creating havoc on earth. With flying citadels called Tripuras that protected him (are they perchance the space stations of today?), he was near-invincible. The only option left for Lord Shiva was to take the form of the mighty Bhima and vanquish this demon. Vanquish he did. But in the fierce battle that ensued, Bhima was made to sweat profusely. And this sweat, it is believed, now runs as river Bhima.

This 18th century temple is built around a swayambhu, or self-created, jyotirling by the Maratha strongman Nana Phadnavis. The ling was impressive, but this impression grew ten-fold when a holy mendicant explained to me the meaning of a shivling. He told me that it's the visual depiction of the divine act of copulation that caused creation, seen from the inside of a woman's body. Much like the view from the camera that's placed inside a tiger's cave by National Geographic.

From the temple town, unlike in all the temples I have seen, you have to descend not ascend, a long flight of steps to reach the temple. And as you take one stone at a time, all along the path you see a veritable gallery of gods guarding the two sides.

Just behind the temple is the trail that takes you to Gupt Bhima or the origin of the Bhima river. Once you get to the river, you walk through the flowing waters till you come to a small waterfall, marked by a smaller shivling, guarded by the sacred bull named Nandi.

While sipping hot tea laced with lemon grass, and savouring the piping hot batata wadas, I saw a priest sitting near me. To avoid the glass that we mere mortals sipped from, he insisted on a 'brand new' plastic glass to sip his holy milk from. And I realized that his misplaced sense of hygiene was detrimental to the environment. Instead of opting for a clean and washed glass that could be 'reused' by all, he chose a 'use-and-throw' glass that will remain an unholy scar on the face of this earth at least for the next 300 years.

From the tea stall, we took the trail to the highest point in Bhimashankar. On the steep climb of over 300 feet, a group of youngsters chided me and my wife saying we won't be able to make it to the top. But both of us were determined to reach the summit of our own little Mount Everest. And we were encouraged by the words of Mike Horn the legendary South African explorer who advised people to never give up on their mission. He said, 'If you can't run, jog. If you can't jog, walk. If you can't walk, crawl. But never, never, never give up.'

The view from the top was absolutely stunning. Undulating mountains capped by majestic peaks in rows after endless rows as far as the eyes could see. It extended left to right, almost like a 70 mm screen. Curtains of clouds hid them for some fleeting moments, and then the peaks reappeared magically, grander than ever. And we realized that we would have missed this magnificent view had we given up the arduous climb half way up the mountain.

The drive back to the beautiful Blue Mormon, the only resort in the middle of nowhere, was through dense patches of forests that cast mottled shadows on the forest road. Without checking in, we drove straight to the sunset point just at the edge of the resort, racing against the setting sun. Gazing at the crimson horizon, I realized that no two sunsets are the same, even from the same sunset point. The angle of the sun changes every day, the cloud formations are distinctly different, and the light is uniquely magical. And as the sun lit up the earth with the passing rays, I marvelled at how this one single ball of fire lights up every single object on this planet, without the help of an additional light. Contrast this with number of lights we need to light up a single house.

It was only the next day morning, standing in the verandah cocooned in our woollens that we discovered that this 175-acre plot has a private helipad, a private lake, and a private jungle trail that takes you to a nearby adivasi village. But the call of the wild was too strong to ignore, and we decided not to tarry any longer at the resort.

The forests at Kondhwal, barely eight kms away, was a butterflying and birding paradise. Just as we entered its precincts, we were welcomed by swarms of blue mormon butterflies. They were basking in the sun to get their wings solar-powered. Once they stocked up energy, they started flitting about from one flower to another. And I started flitting from one butterfly to another, looking for the 'perfect' blue mormon. Being extremely agile, butterflies escape from predators but invariably end up losing a part of their wonderful wings and their symmetry. And we cruel photographers go in search of the 'perfectly symmetrical' butterfly.

At Kondhwal we also saw the elusive shekru or the giant squirrel with its rusty red-and-white fur coat. Highly endangered, it's among the largest squirrels in the world. And measuring all of three feet, it has a tail twice the size of its body, which helps in the balancing act. It makes its nest on the summit of the tallest tree in the neighbourhood and chooses its slenderest branch so that predators cannot walk that delicate path.

Just as we stepped out of the sacred forests of Bhimashankar, my cellphone picked up signal and rudely delivered an unwanted message. That's when it dawned on me that I was totally incommunicado for two full days; and I suddenly felt the unabashed joy of having been 'unreachable'.

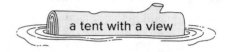

a tent with a view

When we reached the Mollem forest office, we were offered two options. One was to stay at the Rest House right next to the forest office. And the other one was to stay in a tent, bang in the middle of Mollem National Park. Without batting an eyelid, we chose the more romantic option. But it came with a caveat. The jeep would drop us at the campsite and return to base. And we would have to fend for ourselves without a cook as he was on census duty that had just commenced. This meant that for breakfast, lunch and dinner, we would have to walk a mile to the nearest restaurant in Collem village. The path to the village was through a river; and since there was no bridge on the river, we had to wade through knee-deep water every time we ventured into the village. A tricky proposition, especially in the night, as the torch wasn't powerful enough to throw light even on your own feet.

Right outside the tent was a forest clearing which was the meeting place of birds of different feathers. In fact we counted 23 different species taking turns to perch on the trees. Watching this live Animal Planet, we discovered that birds follow a hierarchy and different species perch at different heights on the tree. The basic principle being, the bigger you are the higher you get to perch. A nice little perching order.

The lazy evening was spent at the rivulet that passed through the campsite. The water was shallow enough for one to sit on the riverbed and allow the water to give you a gentle hydro massage. As I lay meditating in the flowing water, I realized why a river is like time. No two moments of a river are the same. It comes from the past, touches the present and flows into the future.

The water that was crystal clear suddenly became muddy, and dried leaves and dried twigs flowed past me. Looking upstream, I discovered the cause. A troupe of monkeys were swinging merrily on the overhanging branches and were happily plunging headlong into the rivulet. Accepting their first right to the river, I retreated to my abode.

The 10 km ride to the famous Dudhsagar waterfall took us through pristine evergreen forests that grew darker and denser by the minute. The jeep crossed the river thrice and stopped at the point from where we had to trek. We walked along the river lined with gigantic black rocks brought crashing down by the relentless river over many millennia.

The sight of the largest waterfall in Goa evoked mixed reactions in me. It was a breathtaking free fall of a thousand feet into an evergreen valley. But this magical fall was cruelly sliced into two by a railway line built by the British in a moment of madness.

On our way back, we stopped by to visit the infamous Devil's Canyon. Here, the water from Dudhsagar river flows through a canyon carved out of treacherous rocks. The water in the canyon is still, almost like a sheet of glass reflecting the blue sky above, inviting. Since there's no board that warns you of an impending death, you are tempted to take a jump. And as you fall prey to your impulse, you are pulled into an unseen whirlpool that drags you through a labyrinth of underwater passages till you reach a point of no return. Many young, unsuspecting lives have been lost here, every year. And it's rumoured that every time a life is lost, it's lost in pairs. And only one old man in the village of Collem can tell you where the bodies will be washed ashore, as only he knows the how the water flows through this maze of underwater tunnels.

After our tryst with the Devil, we returned to the base camp. While crossing the river on our way to Collem for lunch, we were shocked by the legions of picnickers who had descended on the riverbanks from nowhere. They were cooking, eating and drinking. And leaving behind an unsavoury trail of copious consumption. Broken glasses, wrappers, plastic bottles, carry bags, and other assorted litter were being thrown into the ever-forgiving Dudhsagar river. And I silently thanked God for not making a river flow backwards, as all this filth would have flowed back to the breathtaking Dudhsagar waterfalls.

living with the other half

The presiding deity of this tribal village is a goddess called Zakubai. A goddess so powerful that she took it upon herself to protect this village and the nearby four villages, without any help from any of the male gods. She even went to the extent of decreeing that the idols of Hanuman be removed from these five villages. To this day, these five banished idols are kept on the banks of a river near a village called Khadki, all with their faces down. If ever anyone dares to make these idols stand upright, by the morning the idols are found lying flat on their faces again.

Though the village is matriarchal, and is ruled by a tribal goddess, paradoxically it is called Purushwadi. It is said that earlier it was called Pur-unch-wadi, which means the village on top of the mountain. With the gradual onslaught of a male-dominated society, it was conveniently changed to Purushwadi.

This tribal village is about 180 kms from Mumbai. And it's one of the villages adopted by Grassroutes, an organization that has been promoting village tourism in this tribal belt for over four years.

Today, Purushwadi is a picturesque village of 109 houses in which a tribal community called Mahadeo Kolis lives in perfect harmony with Nature. Here again, there is a living paradox. In the very name of the tribe protected by a goddess, a mainstream god has crept in: Mahadeo or Lord Shiva. The fact that these tribals now trek to the Bhairavnath temple situated about 20 kms from here to seek his blessings points to the influence of a mainstream religion on tribal beliefs.

In 2006 only a handful of households joined the Village Tourism Committee. Today over 60 households invite guests to stay with them and experience what it is to live in a village. To make sure that the guests don't experience a culture shock, the housekeepers, the cooks and the guides have been extensively trained.

So the guests, whether they stay in the tents pitched in the wheat fields on the outskirts of the village or in the houses in the village itself, can expect the basics: clean toilets, clean towels, safe water to drink, hot water to bathe, clean mattresses and bedsheets, and even a green salad along with the otherwise authentic, rustic food.

Our host was a lady called Jijabai, whose husband Punaji was a clerk in the Panchayat office. All our meals were cooked and served in this matriarch's house, including the morning tea. I thought the disarming, perpetual smile on her face was because we were her special guests. But as I stepped out of her house into the village, at every corner I saw the same smile on a hundred other faces. And I realized that Mahadeo Kolis are an extremely friendly and warm people. We walked through the narrow lanes of the village as if it was our own village. And the best part was they continued their regular activities, unmindful of our presence: whether they were filling water in their pots, or cutting wood, or harvesting in the wheat fields, or milking their cattle. It was a real slice of life and not a show that was specially put up for us. Much like the Masais of Kenya who have got used to guests coming into their villages; and who live out their life in the open, in front of a hundred inquisitive eyes.

It was at the village square that I meant Datta, an authority on the local flora and fauna. Apart from telling us about the various plants and trees endemic to the area, he also told us about the local varieties of wheat and paddy. And how the import of hybrid seeds into the village had already resulted in three of the endemic rice varieties becoming extinct. Despite the advent of mainstream agriculture, some local species have survived. And whenever someone in the village falls ill, they make sure that only those local species of rice is cooked and served to the patient, till he or she is fully recovered.

Datta also told us about the adverse impact of the government scheme of afforestation. As part of this scheme, the tribals were asked to plant innumerable saplings on a barren hillock. The intentions were noble; but the saplings sadly were of eucalyptus, acacia and jatropa. All of which, when they spread from the hillocks into the unsuspecting farmlands, create havoc with the local plant species, as they guzzle water and deplete the moisture in the soil and reduce the ground water level.

Another interesting character we met was Atmaram, the local expert in honey collection. He is actually a shepherd who goes into the nearby jungles to graze his goats. And as they lazily graze on the grasslands, he follows the busybees to their honeycombs. Village folklore has it that once a tiger attacked his favourite goat, and he grappled with the tiger till he secured his goat's release.

Next up was our trek to the highest point in the region. And on our way to the top, we came across many sacred stones marked in saffron. Made of all shapes and sizes, they were the original idols of the adivasis. An insight into their beliefs was provided by our adivasi guide. When we asked him where the nearest village was, he answered, 'There, right in the belly of that mountain.' Showing that, for an adivasi, a stone is a living thing.

As the sun slowly started dipping behind the Western Ghats, the vast landscape of dried-up grass on the hilltop became a gorgeous tapestry woven with endless golden threads. And when we started our descent, our weary path was lit up by the rising moon, as it was the full-moon night of Holi.

In Purushwadi, everything begins at Zakubai's temple. So did the Holi celebrations. The pyre of dried twigs and small branches was waiting in all readiness. After the temple lamp was lit, young girls lit up their own diyas from the flame of that lamp, and these were in turn used to light up the Holi pyre. Soon, aided by a strong breeze, gigantic tongues of fire leapt into the sky as if to rival the rising moon.

The next day morning we climbed down the mountain slopes lined with mango trees in full bloom to reach the blue river. For a river of its ethereal beauty, it had a phonetically ungainly name: Kurkundi. A dip and a swim in the chilled blue waters did wonders to rejuvenate us and we walked briskly to the village for our breakfast. We had deliberately worn old clothes in anticipation of a colourful Holi ahead. But when we reached the village, there were no pichkaaris, no colour-filled balloons, no bucketsful of vibgyor colours.

That's when it dawned on my urban mind that Rang 'Panchami' is actually meant to be celebrated on the 5th day after the full moon. It's the domination of North Indian culture, perpetrated through Bollywood, that irrevocably changed it to the 2nd day.

Untouched by this, the tribals here were getting ready for five days of festivities packed with various rustic competitions. The first one was to lift one of the three perfectly round boulders that were kept at the village square. And the boulders weighed 25 kgs, 50 kgs, and one that was well over a 100 kgs. This was followed by kabaddi matches, wrestling bouts, and you guessed it right, the mainstream sport: cricket.

As we bid farewell to Jijabai and her family, I really wished this tribe retains its rustic innocence and its very special beliefs and rituals. But the recently-constructed iron bridge that stretches across the river, connecting this tribal village to the mainland, is a grim reminder that mainstream thought will come in by that bridge, by the hour and by the day, and smother the special flavours that have evolved here over many, many centuries. Eventually resulting in the vanillisation of culture, where one flavour suits all.

the hill station inside a fort

Panhala is the lesser-known sister of the three hill stations of Maharashtra. Smaller than Mahabaleshwar but bigger than Matheran, it is the only hill station in the state to be situated bang inside a fort. Nestling in the verdant Sahyadris at a commanding height of 3200 feet, the fort here is spread over all of 8 square kilometres.

Right from the time it was built in the 12th century, it has changed hands as many times as a Bollywood heroine changes costumes in a single song. Built by Raja Bhoj, it was conquered and ruled by the kings of various dynasties: Nagas, Rashtrakoots, Chalukyas, Shilaharas, Yadavas, Palegars, Bahmanis, Adilshahis and Marathas.

You could come to Panhala to see the green glory of the hills and vales that surround this fort, or to hear the stories of valour and sacrifice spoken by the stones and interpreted by a guide.

The list of sacrifices starts from the time of its construction. When the foundation stone of the fort kept caving in, it was suggested that a human sacrifice be made. As this was to be made willingly (it apparently doesn't work if someone is forced), the king went around scouting for volunteers. And a lowly woman called Gangu Taili offered to sacrifice her life. After she agreed, to her horror, she discovered she was pregnant. She asked for time till she delivered her baby, laying down a condition that a part of the fort be named after her baby. It turned out that she delivered triplets, and the three granaries in the Ambarkhana were named after her three daughters: Ganga, Yamuna and Saraswati.

The peak of Panhala's glory was achieved in Shivaji's time. But it also saw the enactment of three of the greatest tragedies witnessed by a fort. It was in the grand Sajja Kothi that Shivaji imprisoned his own son Sambhaji, suspecting him of siding with the enemy. And it was in this fort that one of the most valorous acts of sacrifice ever was lived out. Much before Saddam Hussein could think of creating his look-alikes, Shivaji the master of guerilla warfare had already created one. When the fierce warrior Siddi Johar laid a siege to Panhala with over 1,33,000 soldiers, Shivaji barely had 4,000 soldiers in the fort. He held out for 4 months; but when the granaries became empty, he decided it was time to retreat. He sent out the message of surrender, and as the enemy soldiers waited eagerly he got his dummy Shiva Kashid to travel in the royal palanquin. It was only after they caught the duplicate and executed him brutally that they realised the original had escaped to the nearby Vishalgad.

Another protagonist of this great escape was a valiant soldier, Baji Prabhu Deshpande. When Siddi Johar realized that he had been fooled, he trained his cannons on the original Shivaji. But he ran into the blind courage of a loyal warrior called Baji Prabhu and his equally loyal troop of thirty. On a difficult pass near Pavangad they held fort for an hour laying down their lives one after the other while their beloved original made the great escape.

tanzania's circle of life

As dawn breaks on the endless plains of Serengeti, every lion there wakes up knowing well that it has to run faster than the slowest antelope in sight; and every antelope wakes up knowing for sure that it has to run faster than the fastest lion on the horizon.

The drama of life and death unfolds on the stage of survival, every day and every night, nay every moment. And you realise that the end of a life is only the beginning of another.

When you gaze around the landscape covering all of 360 degrees, you suddenly become conscious of thousands and thousands of zebras and wildebeest slowly closing in on you. And you feel as insignificant as a speck in the dust storm that is created by their gathering hooves. For a moment you feel the same fear that ran through the veins of the prehistoric man till he discovered the cold comfort of a stone-age weapon.

Yes in Serengeti where we witnessed some of Nature's finest spectacles, the land is so flat that Galileo would have thought thrice before declaring the earth is round.

The reason why this landscape is flat goes back a few millennia. A volcanic eruption flattened Serengeti and covered it with ashes so thick that only grass could survive there for centuries on end. And the massive boulders spewed by the volcano landed thousands of miles away and became what's called the kopjes where the lions and lionesses rear their family in quiet privacy.

One of the first sights on our journey was a hyaena's kill. The gazelle was brought down by the lone hyaena. And just as it was preparing for a sumptuous lunch, the hovering vultures got wind of the happening and started descending on the scene, one by one. Within moments, there were over 30 of them, and the hyaena withdrew valiantly from the scene. And for the first time ever, I saw a hyaena with a sheepish grin.

As I saw the starlings flitting by, the secretary bird strutting along, and the white-necked ravens creating a racket, I remembered the pied-crested cuckoo that had flown from Africa all the way to Mumbai to herald the monsoon. The common crows had piled on the poor guest not knowing the Indian hospitality of 'atithi devo bhava'. And in a moment of spontaneous action I 'interfered' with Nature's course and saved the cuckoo and took it all the way to the BNHS office in town. There I handed it over to the caring hands of Isaac Kehimkar who later released it in the BNHS land at Borivli National Park.

How I wish I had ringed that bird to trace its safe journey back to its homeland in Africa. Till date I don't know whether it actually survived the ordeal. I really don't want to know because I want to believe it did.

Then we visited Oldupai where the remains of the earliest man ever to walk the earth was excavated. At that place I felt thirsty. Later I realised that a river had run along there till its course was altered forever by volcanic eruptions. No wonder the recorded memory of a few million years was transmitted in an instant to my parched throat.

The next day was what I call 'National Geographic, Live!' We had booked ourselves for a ride in the hot air balloon. But before we were to see the breathtaking eagle's eye view of the Serengeti grasslands, we were to witness Tanzania in the dying hours of the night. Our trip to the Masai kopjes started at 5 in the morning and we saw glistening eyes lit up by the headlights of our Land Rover. Piercing eyes without accompanying bodies staring straight at us: hippos, jackals, lions, wild hare and hyaenas.

As the balloon manoeuvred by a team of master fliers soared above Serengeti, we saw the aerial view of the most awesome spectacle on earth: the Great Migration.

In May, thousands and thousands of zebras and wildebeest congregate into large groups, building up their cadres to eventually touch an astronomical figure of 20 lakh animals. Come August, they set off on a single trail crossing two violent rivers on the way: the Grumeti and the Mara. And come back all the way back to where they started. In the process losing a few thousand to the fury of the rivers in spate. What makes them undertake this suicidal mission, year after year, is a mystery still to be unravelled by man.

Maybe it is nature's own wanderlust, or maybe it is a journey in which life searches for itself.

Stranger than this masochist ordeal, where they face certain death from the feline predators lying in ambush in the grasslands and the alligators waiting patiently in the swirling rivers, is another tale: The tale of a species of butterflies that migrates all the way from Africa to faraway Canada and comes all the way back. But the twist in the tale is that the lifespan of butterflies being as short-lived as three months, it's the third generation that reaches Canada and the sixth generation that reaches the country of their origin: Africa.

We celebrated our survival and safe landing with a typical champagne breakfast under a flat-top acacia that stood lonely in the grasslands.

There we saw, and tried to make friends with, the calf of a wildebeest that was separated from its mother. Apparently the motherly instincts of the wildebeest is the least developed in the animal kingdom, and consequently mothers losing their calves due to negligence is an hourly occurrence in Serengeti.

When one of the tourists asked whether we could carry it to the safety of civilisation where it could be reared in captivity, our guide Mtaki said sternly,

'Here in the wild only the fittest survive.' And the import of that statement sunk into our souls like a prehistoric rock.

The Great Migration is also linked to the Tale of the Reducing Height of the Grass. At first, the zebras and the wildebeest eat the tall grass thereby reducing its height. Following them are the shorter antelopes like bushbucks that feed on the shortened grass further reducing the height. Last come the tiny gazelles who find the grass perfectly cut to suit their stature.

Yes, Nature has worked it all out. Only one out of 20 attempts by a predator is successful. Which means 19 times the prey gets a chance to die another day. No wonder we saw a cheetah teaching her two grown up calves the fine art of hunting in open plains.

Also, the God who camouflaged the predator also camouflaged the prey: in various shades of the Serengeti brown. Which is probably the reason why we saw leopards take vantage points on top of bare acacia trees to spot the distant movement of preys.

At Lake Manyara, we even saw lions that climb trees. In fact, it's the only place in the world where these special lions are found. Their favourite perches were sausage trees that have branches starting as low as four feet from the ground, enabling an easy climb.

Every day when we crossed a particular patch in the jungle we had to close the hood of our Land Rover and pull up all the window panes as a swarm of 'tse tse' flies would invade the vehicle and inflict really painful bites on our bodies. The yellow fever vaccination that's mandatory for every tourist is to prevent a deadly fever caused by these 'tse tse' flies. It was a gentle reminder that this paradise on earth also has its Pandora's Box.

Then we moved on to Ngorongoro, the largest crater on earth, formed as the volcanic mountains moved away in one giant seismic movement a few millennia ago. Measuring 20 kms in diametre, it's a whole ecosystem that survives inside. There's a mini Tanzania in there: elephants, lions, leopards, hyaenas, zebras, sweet water hippos, salt water flamingos and a plethora of avian species.

But the wildlife that exists inside never really ventures out. So it's almost as if they are marooned in the crater. Only the female elephants move around on the rim of the crater as it's rich in grasslands, and the male elephants with tusks almost touching the ground come to visit them during the mating season.

In the middle of the crater, we witnessed an entire entourage of lions lazing around, yawning and stretching their tired legs. Maybe recharging their batteries after a hard night's work in the wilderness.

As we were driving back to the forest lodge, we saw a double rainbow in the sky spanning the entire crater. Maybe to remind us that we had witnessed a double delight in Tanzania: the endless plains of Serengeti and the marooned mysticism of Ngorongoro.

cottage with a forest

In case you have a deep desire to live inside a forest, and the bigger sanctuaries like Ranthambore, Dudhwa and Tadoba sound a little intimidating, for starters you can try Durshet. It would be your perfect initiation into the Ways of the Forest.

And the best part is, when you book yourself into the cottages of Nature Trails there, you have already got a deal that you hadn't bargained for. It comes with a river, a lake and a forest attached. All for free. The place, unless on an unlucky weekend, is absolutely solitary. So you can safely feel as if you own all these freebies.

Durshet is a friendly forest nestling in the Western Ghats on the banks of river Amba near Khopoli. It's flanked by the Ashtavinayaks of Mahad and Pali. The Varad Vinayak at Mahad is an elegant temple built by the Peshwas at a picturesque location next to a pond. Whereas Ballaleshwar is a temple painted with the most gaudy colours ever imagined by man.

From your doorstep you can watch the changing moods of the majestic Western Ghats; or you can walk down to river Amba and dangle your feet in its gentle waters. And when you are done with the butterfly watching within the complex itself, you can head off for white-water rafting in the river Kundalika, not very far from Durshet. Plus there are adventure sports like rock climbing, river crossing, rappelling – all at an arm's distance.

The most wonderful thing about these adventure sports is that it's your own humble version of Man v/s Wild. At the end of each event, you feel the immense joy of having conquered Nature. Or is it actually yourself?

But for us, the highpoint of the trip was the jungle trek in the night. We set off after dinner into the moonless forest, the lone beam of the guide's torch lighting up the pathless land.

The entire forest was enveloped in dense darkness. The sky was starlit; but I realised that even a thousand stars can't make up for the missing full moon.

The creatures of the night were making their presence felt with their eerie calls: the owls, the night jars and the occasional jackal.

The hunt for the tarantula spider drew a blank but the torchlight caught a blacknaped hare that darted across us in sheer fright. It was difficult to say who was more scared: us or the hare.

Suddenly the forest became silent; even the cicadas stopped midway into their nightsong. And I was reminded of the time when I witnessed a solar eclipse in the forests of Nagzira in Maharashtra. It was late afternoon and the forest was alive and vibrant. The moment the sun was covered by the eclipse, the entire forest became silent as if night had fallen. When the eclipse passed and the sun regained its lost glory, the forest became alive again. And the denizens of the forest would have wondered how the night lasted for just twenty minutes.

As we stood at the edge of darkness and stared at the Durshet valley below, I remembered that distant night in Tadoba sanctuary when we were doing night census of the wildlife there. After the range officer dropped us to the machaan overlooking the waterhole, the first sighting we had was of a mama bear carrying a baby bear on her back. They passed by right under our shaky machaan. And when we moved a wee bit in sheer fright, the creaking of the loose wooden plank on which we were sitting reverberated in the pindrop silence of the forest. We were mortified that the bear would look up and spot us. But it went away having better things to do. On that lonely night that seemed to have no dawn, we spotted many animals that ventured to quench their thirst at the waterhole that was drying up by the hour: a lone leopard, a troupe of langurs, a couple of porcupines, a pack of wild dogs, and even a peacock that was suffering from a bad case of insomnia.

When we returned to the safety of the well-lit cottage, we realised an eternal truth that the caveman would have realised many eons ago: darkness is fear and light is courage.

blue sky and blue waters

There is a fort called Vasota nestling in the green mountains deep inside the Koyna sanctuary. Protected by deep gorges all around and guarded by ferocious tigers that roamed the valley, it was once upon a time near-inaccessible. Though it was built by Raja Bhoj, it was conquered by the Marathas. At the peak of Maratha power, a few Englishmen were kept prisoners here. Subsequently, the Marathas lost the Anglo-Maratha War of 1818. But the news of defeat took two years to travel to this fort. And the poor Englishmen had to continue their life as prisoners for two long years despite winning the war.

When a dam was built on the confluence of the three rivers, Koyna, Solshi and Kandati, the inaccessible forest suddenly became accessible: Because the backwaters of the dam stretched for all of 65 kilometres encircling the mountains like watersnakes. Now you can enter this sanctuary only by boat from Shivsagar Lake.

We set off from our base in Tapola and took the necessary permission from the range officer in Bamnoli. And the forest guard accompanied us on our 45-minute boat journey to the sanctuary.

Koyna by summer and Koyna by winter are two completely different landscapes. Post monsoon, the deep gorges get filled with rainwater and the water level rises over 600 feet, and the boat can be anchored right at the forest gate. Since we made our trip in summer and the water level was just about a 100 feet, the boat had to be moored far away and we had to make an arduous journey of about two kms over loose boulders strewn all along the path.

As we approached the forest gate, we saw a herd of animals which we mistook for the aggressive bisons. But on a second look, the white socks that's the distinctive identity of bisons was missing. And we realized that they were just 'feral' buffaloes. A special category of domestic buffaloes that stray into a forest and decide to make it their adopted home.

We took the path to Vasota fort and soon chanced upon the pugmarks of the elusive pangolin or the ant-eater. The guard explained a unique characteristic of this strange-looking animal that has hard, wooden scales on its body. When threatened, it has the habit of rolling into a rock-like ball thus making it impregnable to man or beast.

Then we walked under dense overhanging boughs through a tunnel of blue butterflies, and this added an ethereal touch to our walk. Each step of ours on the dried up forest floor caused panic among the butterflies. That was when the guard demonstrated the art of walking on dried leaves without making a sound. The trick, he told us in a whisper, is to land the heel first and then the rest of the foot. And presto, soon we were walking as if in a silent movie.

When we settled down near a Ganesh temple in the middle of nowhere, a barking deer darted across with its distinctive dog-like bark. The packed spartan lunch of chapathi and egg burji was washed down with water from the cool mountain stream, and we started on our journey back. By then we had realized that we had stopped once too often to stare at the wondrous woods, and we couldn't possibly reach Vasota and return by dusk by which time the park gate would have been closed.

Sitting in the boat that was chugging back to the madding crowd in Tapola, I wondered if the recent crown of a World Heritage Site bestowed upon the Western Ghats by UNESCO is going to make any difference to the fragile fate of Koyna. There are allegations of forest land having been sold to resort owners, and windmills having been set up in the corridors of animal migration; and the matter was sub-judice. Add to this the promotion of Tapola as the New Mahabaleshwar to decongest the well-known hill station that's just 25 kms away. Will the decongestion of Mahabaleshwar result in the congestion and eventual destruction of the natural treasures of Koyna? Mother Nature knows.

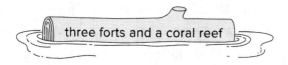

three forts and a coral reef

Gigantic rocks that float in the middle of the sea have always fascinated me. Especially the ones that have been carved into sea forts. In the course of a long, arduous journey I discovered three of them. And as a just reward for all my efforts, I stumbled upon a coral reef right behind one of them.

The first of these was the fort of Janjira. Standing on the shifting sands of Murud beach, I gazed at the Arabian Sea and mistook the sea fort in front to be the invincible Janjira. But a fisherman on the beach told me that it was a fort called Padmadurg. Built by Sambhaji, it was meant to be the answer to the might of Janjira. But it turned out to be so weak that it was sliced into three desolate pieces by the cannons of the Siddis.

From the nearby Rajapur jetty, I took a boat to the fort of Janjira. It was a large catamaran that could easily carry up to 40 people. And it had large, flapping sails that were torn over time by the fury of the sea wind. As six boatmen struggled to get the sails up, and then to steady the boat that was pitching and rolling in the pre-monsoon wind, I marvelled at the indomitable spirit of the seamen of yesteryears.

It was on a stormy night in the 17th century that a ship carrying spice traders from Africa was washed ashore by tidal waves. When the local King of Murud, Rajaram Patil, refused to give them shelter, these fierce and fearless warriors called Siddis took it forcibly. They decided to stay put in Murud and have been here for three centuries; and the present Siddi Nawab of Murud continues to live in his palace on the hilltop.

Near this palace in a place called Gol Gumbaz are the tombs of the early Siddi rulers. Folklore has it that buried under these tombs is a treasure that can last twelve generations. The only catch in unearthing this treasure is that the person who digs it up should be able to read the Quran backwards without a pause. In case the gold digger doesn't meet this simple criterion, he will have to face the curse of instant death or lasting madness.

The fort of Janjira stands 90 feet tall above the sea and 22 feet under. It took 22 years to build, is spread over 22 acres, and has 22 bastions to defend it. It's considered 'ajinkya' or inconquerable, as innumerable attacks were launched on it by the British, the Portuguese, and by the Marathas led by Shivaji, Kanhoji, Chimaji and Sambhaji – but all of them had to invariably beat a hasty naval retreat.

This fort is believed to have been built not as a naval base but as a structure to protect a Sufi saint named Peer Panchatan Baba, who used to sit and meditate on this rocky island. The first sight that you come across when you enter the fort is his tomb. And the guide in a hushed whisper tells you that the power of the saint is undiminished till date. During the height of monsoon even today, tidal waves rise up to 40 feet in the sea but when they enter the fort their height is reduced to 20 feet, and they miraculously stop at his feet. A mystical occurrence or an engineering marvel, one wonders.

Suvarnadurg, the second sea fort in my list, was off Harnai, arguably the busiest port on the coast of Konkan. With every country boat in sight involved in either trading their wares or in auctioning the catch of the night, I scanned the horizon for a friendly and willing boatman who would row me across to the fort floating in the sea. And I met an old man in the sea, too old to go for fishing, but too young to give up rowing. He readily agreed and we set sail. Looking at the camera slung across on my shoulder, he asked me gingerly if I would like to see dolphins. And without waiting for my answer, he changed course and headed straight into the deep sea.

There was no sign of them anywhere, but his instinct guided his oars. Suddenly, out of the blue sea there appeared one, nay two, frolicking dolphins. And they kept disappearing and appearing at will. They were so unpredictable that not once could I click a half-decent picture. To make matters worse, every time they surfaced they had a benign smile on their faces, as if telling me, 'Fooled you again!'

The boat soon landed on the shimmering white sands of the beach at the edge of Suvarnadurg. The main entrance to the fort was so well camouflaged that you don't see it till you are at a cannon ball's distance. As I got down into the shallow waters, I saw the sight of a white-bellied sea eagle swooping down on a fish that had come up for a breath of fresh air. That turned out to be its last breath.

Built by the King of Bijapur in the 16th century and conquered by Shivaji in the 17th, this is the fort that launched a thousand naval battles. And it was from here that the legendary naval admiral of the Marathas, Kanhoji Angre, repulsed a virulent attack by the Siddis of Murud.

The famed guerilla strategy of the Marathas is evident in the very structure of this fort. It's replete with a maze of escape routes called 'Chor Darwazas'. Soldiers would retreat through these routes, reach the mainland through a sea tunnel and ask for additional reinforcements. Thus was won many a naval battle in Suvarnadurg.

The last of the forts was Sindhudurg, the jewel in the crown of the Maratha Empire. Built under the personal supervision of Shivaji, it's a fort of immense strength. Its foundation is laid in solid lead, and its walls are reinforced with 1500 tonnes of iron. But despite being an architectural marvel, it could never be consecrated as the naval headquarters of the Maratha Empire because of the curse of a local priest.

Inside the fort, you can literally see the lasting impression left behind by Shivaji. His footprints and handprints have been preserved here in limestone for posterity. Another unique thing about this fort is that there is a temple where Shivaji himself is the deity. As you walk into the sanctum sanctorum and look at the idol, you realize that the idol looks less like the Shivaji you know and more like his Malvani cousin.

But the best part of the journey was kept for the last. The enthusiastic boatman-guide took me on a round trip of the rocky island, and to my utter disbelief I saw the amazing sight of impeccable beaches laced with white, sparkling sand, all around the island. And right behind the fort was the most pristine of them all, with coral reefs submerged in the turquoise blue waters. As I chanced upon a family snorkelling near a coral reef, the world shrunk by a thousand miles, and right in front of me, right on the coast of Konkan, I saw the breathtaking beauty of the Andamans.

lonavala rewind

Once upon a time, Lonavala used to be deserted in the monsoons. The only people you would accidentally run into at the Bushi Dam would be people from your own group. The only scream of joy you would hear at the cascading waterfall at Tiger's Leap would be the echo of your own scream. And the only footsteps you would hear apart from those of yours would be those of the goats that were climbing alongside you. That was in the 70s.

If you are in your 50s and want to rewind back to those times, or if you were not even a twinkle in your parents' eyes way back in the 70s and want to know what life was like then, take the road to Lonavala but don't stop there. Go towards Pune on the old highway for another 15 kms passing Karla till you reach a dusty crowded village called Kamshet. Don't be disappointed; hold your courage. When you turn left from here, the world metamorphoses into an idyllic, rustic landscape after just 3 kms. And from there on it's a journey back in Time Machine.

A vast expanse of paddy fields and sunflower fields open up before you, and you will see farmers working almost in slow motion. Looking at them you will not believe they are the descendants of the fearsome guerilla warriors of King Shivaji: the maavlas.

It was late morning and the sunflowers were all facing the east, like disciplined soldiers in a parade. And I remembered my childhood belief that a sunflower faces the east at sunrise and keeps turning its head in the direction of the sun till it ends up facing the west at sunset. I don't know if it's true and I don't really care. Because beautiful stories should be left just as they are. As beautiful stories.

On the way to Kondeshwar temple atop the mountain, I saw two more architectural marvels of Nature: the nest of the harvester ant and the nest of the pagoda ant. The former makes a nest on the ground. At first glance it looks like the sand sculpture of a flower. The petals of this flower are so angled as to light up the inside of the nest, every passing moment from sunrise to sunset. And on every single day of the year. The harvester ants 'harvest' seeds from the forest, peel them, and store them inside this 4-feet deep nest saving them for a rainy day.

The nest of the pagoda ant on the other hand is made on a tree. First the ant converts the bark of the tree into a fine powder and then after mixing it with its saliva painstakingly makes a nest that resembles a pagoda. The nest actually looks like an ant-eater hanging upside down. And thereby hangs a tragic tale too. Some species of woodpecker get attracted to this ready-made nest and they start pecking into it. Once a hole is made, the female woodpecker enters it and lays its eggs. And once the eggs hatch and the fledglings come out, the mother feeds them with the hosts: the pagoda ants. Talk about eating the hand that feeds you!

Still trying to decode the ways of Nature, I reached the temple of Kondeshwar. A priest who didn't look like a priest greeted me. When he came to know that I'm from Mumbai, he fondly remembered the time he was part of an ilk famous for their coding and decoding: the dabbawalas. After 5 years in the profession, he came back to his native temple and took over as the priest from his father. He pointed out to a live termite mound inside the temple, and said in a hushed whisper, 'The serpent that guards the temple lives there.' Once again, I didn't ask for proof. I believed him just like I believed the story of the sunflower.

Haribhau (that was his name) then took me to a 3-tiered waterfall just behind the temple. From there we walked to a clearing flanked by towering cliffs on either side. To the left was the trail of the gruelling trek to Bhairi Caves high up in the clouds.

Then I drove back to Kamshet village past a landscape adorned with a patchwork of lovely lakes, bisected the highway, and went towards the inviting waters of Pavna Dam. The road took me through Bor Ghat which was an exact replica of the Khandala Ghat of yesteryears. As the ghat began, a temple appeared bang in the middle of the road; and drivers of passing vehicles were seen chucking coins in the direction of the temple hoping for temporary blessings that will last at least till the ghat is crossed.

When I got down at Pavna and walked towards the lake, a startled red-wattled lapwing took off into the sky, and hovered around my head, screaming continuously. I must have inadvertently gone near its nest. A lapwing doesn't make a nest, but lays its eggs among the pebbles, so perfectly camouflaged that only she can tell the eggs from the stones. I steered away from the spot and the bird quietened down, assured of the safety of its next generation.

As I drove back, a cool breeze applied a soothing balm over the sunburns of the day. And once again I was reminded of the quiet drive back to Mumbai, along the quiet highway of the 70s.

When I was 20, my nostalgic memories were of my childhood. At 54, it is the Lonavala of my teens. And I realized that nostalgia isn't what it used to be. It had grown older.

on the blackbuck trail

Flashback. Karnataka. Circa 1993.

The very first time I went looking for blackbucks turned out to be a wild goose chase. On my journey to Kerala by road, a signboard that said 'Way to Ranebennur Blackbuck Sanctuary' waylaid my plans. And I set off in the direction of the arrow. But even after driving for a good 30 kms, there was no sign of any Blackbuck Sanctuary, leave alone a blackbuck. After another 5 kms and many discreet enquiries, I came across a board that announced my destination in big bold letters: 'Ranebennur Blackbuck Sanctuary'. But below it was written in smaller type: 'Proposed'. So much for the fine print in wildlife signages.

Flashback. Maharashtra. Circa 2002.

The very first encounter with the most beautiful of all Indian antelopes was in the only blackbuck sanctuary in Maharashtra: Rehekuri. This was a tiny island of grassland floating in the midst of farmlands where blackbucks lived, cut off from the nearest herd by a few hundred miles.

Out in the scrubby grassland I saw the first group grazing with their calves. Slowly the numbers in the herd increased till in one group it reached a staggering thirty. And I was told by the guide that their population had almost trebled in the last seven years. But naturalists warn that increasing numbers in the wild is not always a healthy sign. It's actually the health of the herd that truly matters. Rehekuri is a teenie-weenie sanctuary of just 2 sq kms, completely cut off from other forests. So practically these animals are marooned on this island, and thus prone to inbreeding. This naturally results in weaker offspring. And to make matters worse, there are no predators here to make sure only the fittest survive.

Flashback. Rajasthan. Circa 2009.

Jodhpur, the home of many Bishnois, offered me a different spectacle altogether. In the villages here, namely Khejadli, Rotu, Jajiwal and Samrathal, blackbucks coexist with humans in perfect harmony. The Bishnois revere them, keeping vessels filled with water near their houses for them, and even allowing them free access to their ready-to-harvest farms. In fact, a Bishnoi farmer in Jajiwal told me with utmost equanimity, 'Whatever is left in the farms by the blackbucks is what belongs to us'.

In Khejadli, I met Dr. Sumit Dookia who has been researching the relationship between blackbucks and the Bishnois for over a decade. He had a pertinent observation to make. He said that the blackbucks living in and around Bishnoi villages behave differently from those in the wild. Firstly they have started believing that all human beings are Bishnois, and that has put them at tremendous risk especially with poachers. Another change is in the mating rituals. Compared to the elaborate rituals in the real wild, here in the villages they are short and curtailed.

But these are insignificant details when compared to the yeomen's service this community has rendered to mankind by conserving an entire ecosystem. Dr. Sumit shared with me an interesting fact: There are more blackbucks and chinkaras in Bishnoi villages than in all the wildlife sanctuaries of Rajasthan put together.

Velavdar, Gujarat. Circa 2014.

The best place to see blackbucks in their natural glory is Velavdar Blackbuck Sanctuary in Southern Gujarat. With rolling grasslands stretching up to 32 sq kms, it's our own mini Africa. Nowhere else in India can you find endless grasslands with hundreds of a single species grazing all at once.

At the last count there were over 1,600 blackbucks inside the sanctuary, and around 3,000 outside, in nearby protected areas extending up to another 25 kms. In fact, a few corridors have been specifically left open for them to migrate, in case of over-population.

It was evening when we reached the forest guest house. Dumping my luggage, I jumped into the jeep of the affable Devji Waghela, the range officer in charge. The very first sighting was of jackals, the natural predators of blackbuck, who ensure only the fittest of them survive. Then we witnessed a typical Bollywood romance scene. A majestic male blackbuck was trying to woo the female who pretended she's least interested. After many romantic sequences she relented; and the shy blades of grass leaned towards each other in a symbolic gesture!

By then it was time for the sun to set, and the blackbucks decided to call it a day. There were many divergent groups: a couple of nuclear families, some joint families, a few harems, some bachelor parties, and a few groups of rejected males.

But when they settled down to sleep, four members from each group decided to have their forty winks facing in four different directions. They were the guards for the night, who would warn the group of any attack by predators under the cover of night.

It indeed was a moonless night. Thousands of stars had pierced holes in the black canopy of the night, and light years were peeping in through them.

The next morning the sun rose from the east and the blackbucks rose from the grasslands. From the eastern side, hordes of them crossed over to the western side, bisecting a dirt track. But for some inexplicable reason, each one of them would pause for a split second on the track and then spring across the track in boundless joy. They are the fastest animals on earth after the cheetah, and can cover a distance of 20 feet in one single leap of joy.

Ayub, our guide for that day, took us to a place guided by his sixth sense. And right enough we spotted a striped hyaena with jaws strong enough to crush a thigh bone. He was happily feeding on the left-overs of last night.

At Velavdar, the dreaded Ganda Baawal or the Insane Babool has been kept on a tight leash by the forest department by uprooting it whenever it rears its ugly, green head. This weed-tree, the seeds of which were imported from Australia and aerially sprayed across Kachchh to increase its green cover a couple of decades ago, has created havoc in Gujarat. And the green cancer has now spread up to Punjab in the North and Karnataka in the South, suffocating the local vegetation and slowly wiping them out.

As the evening descended, so did the dark clouds pregnant with rain. A large, white egret cut through the gathering storm with effortless ease. And then it poured. The smell of barren earth as she got drenched was enchanting. No perfume in the world can match this heady fragrance, much as they may try to bottle it.

call of the sea

When I think of Kolis, I remember that distant morning when Rajaram Mahulkar first took me to discover flamingos. At that time Mahul was a sleepy village that had just woken up to the fact that beautiful birds with wings of fire had landed on its shores for the very first time. Armed with a pair of binoculars, we set sail in Rajaram's fishing boat and in a while saw them in the distance. An endless line of pink feathers feeding on the blue-green algae along the mangroves of Mahul.

Rajaram was so enamoured by the spectacle that he became the local guardian of these winged visitors, reporting for the past 18 years any harm that's being done to them or to their fragile habitat. And he has remained my friend too; because when a Koli makes a friend, he makes it for a minimum of a lifetime.

Kolis believe in living in the moment. So they celebrate life, singing their famous Koli songs and dancing to their own tune as if there's no tomorrow. This is particularly poignant because when a Koli ventures into the sea, there's really no guarantee of him seeing the dawn of tomorrow. For him every day is a fight for survival, battling the vagaries of the sea, miles away from the safety of the shore.

Rajaram makes it a point to invite me for their annual Koli Utsav, which I never miss. Because for me it's the very celebration of the transient nature of life itself.

I set out from Mumbai to meet more of Rajaram's ilk along the Konkan coast. It was a long journey of over 600 kilometres along an unexplored coast dotted with colourful fishing boats bobbing in the sea.

My first halt was Versoli, an unknown village tucked away between the known villages of Kashid and Alibaug, about a 100 kilometres from Mumbai.

It's at Versoli that I discovered that every fishing boat is so uniquely painted that it becomes the signature of the owner. The beach here is secluded as the only access is through the meandering lanes of the Koliwada. As you walk to the beach, you see fish being dried to ensure a steady supply when fishermen refrain from going to the sea during the monsoon. This vacation ensures two things: safety for the fishermen during the treacherous monsoon; and ample time for the fishes to multiply as they only breed during that time of the year.

As you gaze into the sea at Versoli, you see the Kolaba fort on one side, and the twin forts of Khanderi and Undheri on the other. When I asked a fisherman if he could row me across to one of the forts, he flatly refused. The reason being, a large shoal of shrimp has just been sighted in the sea and all the boats were rushing there in a state of absolute emergency. And I knew that when it comes to making important decisions in life, the Kolis have their priorities absolutely clear.

Korlai was a different experience. Here was a community of about a thousand fisherman who spoke a dialect unique to them: Portuguese Creole. It's a dialect that has become extinct in the erstwhile Portuguese colonies like Daman & Diu. But it has thrived here for 260 years, thanks to their insulation from the rest of the world. Hope this dialect, and the other 1427 dialects spoken in our country, survive the onslaught of mainstream linguistic influences. Because, as a famous linguist mourning the death of an Andamanese dialect said, 'When a dialect becomes extinct, humanity loses a part of itself.'

Despite the dialect that makes them unique, the fishermen of Korlai share universal similarities with the rest of the fishing community along the Konkan coast: Their faith in the Goddess of the Sea, or Jal Maayee as they lovingly call her, who they believe will bring them back safely from the fickle-minded sea. And the love and care with which they build their boats, and keep them in a state of permanent sea-worthiness.

Korlai is surrounded by the sea on three sides, and the small beach for them is an extension of their village. Which is what all beaches were; till picnickers usurped them as their own. Here, in Korlai, there is not a footprint that's not of the fishermen and their families. And looking at its pristine nature, I prayed that if ever anyone discovers this beach and treads on it, let it be as a guest. Fully aware that it should be left as he or she had first found it. Pristine.

Kelus, near Vengurla on the Southern tip of the Konkan coast, was the next stop. Here I saw an auction for the first time, where a fisherman proudly laid bare his catch of the day and offered it to the highest bidder. This fishing village is situated between the river and the deep sea. And during monsoon, the river is in spate and the sea is in fury. In preparation for the onset of monsoon, I saw large bunds being built to break the gigantic waves that lash the seashore. But, in the past, such efforts have only given a symbolic reassurance to the fisherfolk of Kelus. The sea, which seems to have a mind of its own, eventually has its violent way.

Here I also witnessed the intricate art of making large dragnets. The way the dexterous hands of the fishermen wove a net out of nothing reminded me of Samuel Johnson. He had once infamously described a fishing net as 'many holes that have been stitched together.'

At the nearby fishing village of Nivti, the climax of my journey was awaiting me. An affable fisherman named Arvind Maittar had agreed to take me for deep sea fishing.

When I reached there, the uniqueness of the beach caught my attention. Where the beach ended, a creek began. The fishermen moored their fishing boats in this creek, each one in his allotted parking lot. Arvind told me that the fishermen of Nivti go fishing only in the night as they believe that the fish can see a dragnet during the day and will diligently avoid it. So he had warned me that we may not catch any fish as it was only late afternoon. We set sail from the jetty, and soon the safety of the shore looked distant. To take my mind away from the fear of the unknown waters, Arvind pointed to the Nivti fort floating in the sea. Next to it was a pair of dolphins diving in and diving out at will. Like the sea, they were unpredictable. You just couldn't guess where they would appear next.

Arvind then showed me a rocky island in the sea and told me the story of Bandaar Kada. There are massive caves in those rocks, both above and below sea level, where thousands of swift birds nest. A decade ago, some outsiders got wind of it, and the word spread with the sea breeze. And then started the wanton destruction of the nests that were made from the saliva of these birds. And tonnes and tonnes of these nests were smuggled into China and other countries in the Far East where a Swift Nest Soup is a cruel delicacy. Local fisherman from Nivti reported this to the authorities and a raid by the Wildlife Department put a stop to this gruesome act. Today, regular monitoring is done by both the local guardians of these birds, along with naturalists and wildlife officials.

As the boat entered the deep sea, Arvind and his friend picked up the huge dragnet from the bottom of the boat, and slowly opened it out. When it got entangled, he patiently undid the complicated knots. Then in a choreographed move, they cast the net and waited, and waited, and waited. As I looked around, I could only see water, water, everywhere. An inexplicable fear came over me; and I felt helpless and humbled by the power of the elements. Suddenly the boat became a little unsteady, and our hearts missed a combined beat. Arvind calmly told me it's time to turn back. He and his friend quickly pulled up the net, and as he had predicted, there was no fish in the net, except a single, slender fish called the silver fish. Since it made no sense to carry this lone fish back with us, Arvind in a gesture of magnanimity threw it back into the sea. For it to die another day.

And as the dark, pre-monsoon clouds gathered ominously in the skies, and the wind picked up a frightening force, the helpless boat started tossing and turning in the sea. With a prayer on his lips and a steely resolve in his heart, Arvind rowed me back to the safety of the shore. To live another day. And to tell this tale.

the missing hill station

When the British scanned the Indian topography, they didn't miss an inch. And they converted the most scenic of all locations, nestling atop majestic mountains, into hill stations. Just so that they could chill there during the oppressing tropical summers. And they named the various points in these hill stations after British aristocracy: Lodwick Point, Wilson Point, Arthur's Seat, Babington Point, Kate's Point etc.

But the point is, they missed one hill station: Saputara. So here you find a hill station with a 'desi' flavour. No Raj hangover (that would have been a difficult proposition in any case in Dry Gujarat), no colonial mansions, and no points and alleys named after British aristocracy.

Though it's the only hill station in Gujarat (Mount Abu has been adopted by Gujarat as its own but actually it falls in Rajasthan), it's much less hyped when compared to the Lonavalas, the Matherans and the Mahableshwars of the world. In fact it's so small, you can walk into yourself at the next turn.

Situated at a breathtaking height of around 3,000 feet, it's the second highest plateau in the entire Sahydaris. It too has many points; but they are innocently named as Sunset Point, Sunrise Point, Echo Point and Town View Point. But not to be outnamed by the British, one of the points has been patriotically named Gandhi Shikhar.

In Saputara, everything centres around the lake. And that offers an innocuous pleasure: boating. But the ripples of excitement that your paddle creates spread all around the lake and engulf the entire plateau.

Close by, there are forests that you can explore. It's rumoured that Ram spent 11 out of his 14 years of exile in the neck of these woods. But when you walk here, you would agree that it's not really such a bad place to be exiled to.

After you have your fill of the wild, you can turn your attention to places where Nature has been tamed. Beautiful plants that would have grown wild in the wild have been pruned and shaped into submission. Come to think of it, in a way, manicuring a garden is actually cruelty to plants. Because instead of letting them be, you decide what shape they should take, to what height they should grow, and even where they should be placed. But birds and butterflies, blissfully unaware of the tragedy that has befallen their brethren, continue to abound in large numbers in these gardens: Lake Garden, Step Garden, Rose Garden and the Millennium Garden.

Saputara got its name from the tribals who live nearby: the Warlis, the Bhils and the Gamits. Every year on Nagpanchami day, they descend into the nearby Sarpaganga River to worship the serpents here. Hence the name 'Saputara'. Till I heard this story, I believed it's because of the serpentine roads that you traverse to reach this paradise.

The Tribal Museum here offers a glimpse into their lives and times and showcases their amazing artistry: ornaments, paintings, masks, wood carvings, musical instruments and exquisite bamboo craft.

Saputara in winter looks like a secret that is covered in an enigma that is wrapped in a mystery.

One of the most mysterious sights here is the waterfall on the Gira River. When you go near it and gaze at the cascading water you realize that no two moments of the waterfall are the same. The water that falls here every moment, like time, will never come back. It will only go forward to meet the eventual sea. And this water must have started its perennial journey when Mother Earth was born and will continue to flow through her veins till her very last breath.

a green dream

When a journalist named D. M. Mohite visited the famed Tadoba sanctuary in 1970, he was amazed by the way this forest was being nurtured and protected. And he remembered with sadness how an entire forest in his native village of Devrashtra in Maharashtra was being destroyed by the wanton felling of trees and the insatiable grazing of cattle.

Instantly he saw a vision of the dry mountain slopes in his village being nursed back into the green of health. But it took him 15 tenacious years to convince the villagers and the powers-that-be to actually do it.

This forest is called Sagareshwar Sanctuary, and it's the only man-made sanctuary in India where all the animals have been re-introduced.

The first thing Mohite did after he came back to his village was to get the villagers to agree to stop the grazing of cattle. Then, with shramadaan, he and the villagers planted thousands of indigenous saplings across the length and breadth of this degraded forest. For years, they carried water from the nearby villages up the hillock and tended to them with love and care. Once these saplings grew up to be young trees, wild animals were brought in with the help of the forest department: sambar deer, spotted deer, blackbuck, fox, wild boar, snakes, mongoose and porcupine. Birds and butterflies just breezed in.

This forest is also a rare example of continuous upgradation by the forest department over the last three decades. First it was declared a deer park, then a forest reserve, and then a wildlife sanctuary. It is fenced all around, except for the animal migration corridors. And all this happened when Mohite was still around.

We reached there on a Tuesday, and fortunately the park is closed to casual visitors on Tuesdays. So we had the entire guest house to ourselves, as also the forest. And it's truly a great feeling when you have 10 square kms of forest all for yourselves.

Though there were over a 100 species of birds here, the national bird was conspicuous by its presence. A loud call welcomed us, and as we walked to the first waterhole we saw them in all moods and poses: some on treetops with their bronze feathers glistening in the morning light; some busy pecking on the morning dew; some perfecting their majestic 'rain' dance; and some gliding down from their perches and leaving behind a streak of ultramarine blue.

But Mohan Karnat, the Chief Conservator of Forests, Kolhapur, shared with us a stunning ecological truth: a spurt in the numbers of peacocks is not a good sign for the habitat. Simply because, being voracious eaters they polish off copious quantities of newly sprouted grass, thereby destroying the grasslands. In the true wild, this balance is maintained by predators.

Then we saw plum-headed parakeets, green barbets called veda raaghu for their insane flight pattern, hoopoes, crested larks, and a whole colony of baya weaver birds.

A walk in the forest here is enough to convince you that this is an ideal place for eco-tourism. Probably that's why Mohan Karnat and his dedicated team of S. Zhure and S. Naykal are busy setting up a cluster of beautifully designed cottages, a nature interpretation centre, and an amphitheatre to screen wildlife films so that visitors are sensitized to the forest and all that dwells in it.

Situated at a height of 2700 feet, the scenic Sagareshwar is probably the only wildlife sanctuary that has 'points' like in a hill-station. So you have the Ranshool Point, the Kirloskar Point and the Mahangund Point.

As we were trekking up the mountain, I realized the pressures of tourism on this tiny sanctuary. Inside the forest is the Lingeshwar temple that's the twin-brother of the Sagareshwar temple outside. So any devotee who visits

Sagareshwar feels that he hasn't collected enough blessings and makes it a point to visit Lingeshwar to collect some more. Just to give you an idea, the day before we reached here was the last Monday of the month of Shraavan, and the sanctuary log showed an entry of, hold your breath, 28,963 visitors! Signs of their devotion were littered all over the place and over 20 people had to work nonstop to tidy up. In fact, our guide Dokle and a young lady forest guard Devki were collecting the trash missed by the earlier team even as they were spotting the birds and the bees for us.

In the evening we drove down to Mohityanche Vadgaon, named after the progenitor of this sanctuary, Mohite. The idea was to spot the blackbucks that one fine morning had decided to migrate to this village through the gaps in the fence of the sanctuary. They had moved here a few years ago and never came back. We did find two groups of blackbucks on the fringes of the farmlands. Maybe they came here looking for their alpha male, Mohite. And are still looking for him.

a leap of faith

Circus has changed dramatically. During my childhood (and that was a very long time ago), circus was a grand spectacle that paraded a plethora of wild animals tamed by the whip of the ringmaster: tigers, lions, seals and hippopotamus. I still remember the palpitations of my tiny heart as the lion opened its mouth wide and the ringmaster in a valiant gesture stuck his head into the lion's gaping mouth. But to my teenaged wonder, the lion did not snap its mouth shut.

Thankfully the ban on making wild animals perform has brought down their long list to just elephants. On the reasoning that elephants are tamed to perform menial tasks and in temple festivals, they continue to be found in circuses. In Kohinoor Circus they were found playing cricket and even performing an elaborate pooja of Lord Shiva.

Probably the ban on animals was a blessing in disguise. Because the focus of the circus then inevitably shifted to the exhibition of incredible human feats, created with imagination and executed with supreme skill.

The circus continues to fascinate me. Inside that imposing tent there still exists a heady mix of magic, music, dance, jugglery, acting and showmanship. They roll out in clockwork precision, relentlessly for a breathtaking 150 minutes.

Of all the circus feats that I had witnessed in my childhood, a few vestiges still remain in today's circus: the well of death where a motorcyclist rides a bike in vertical circles; the drunken clown who performs immaculate feats on a galloping horse; the cycle that breaks into innumerable pieces when the clown mounts it; and the fire-eater who performs with amazing dexterity. And even today, people continue to applaud the same feats with the same childlike exuberance and innocent joy. Proving that despite the overt changes that have happened around us, human beings haven't changed at heart. We still laugh at the same things, cry for the same things, and of course worry about the same things.

My rekindled curiosity took me to meet Raja Hussain, the young manager of Kohinoor Circus, now tented on the outskirts of Navi Mumbai. He told me how difficult it has become for a circus to survive. Three decades ago, there were over 900 circus troupes in the country. Today, there are less than a 100 left. Just like the animals that once used to grace the circus, the circus too has become an endangered species.

As I was speaking to Raja, I realized the sheer logistical nightmare of running a circus. In a single troupe, there are over 250 people living in the tents that dot the periphery of the performing tent. This includes artistes, carpenters, masons, electricians, tailors, cooks, managers and innumerable helping hands. A mini township of sorts. Apart from managing interpersonal relationships, their daily needs and basic amenities have to be taken care of. And since the circus is a 365-day affair, there is not even a break to set things right in case something goes wrong. The circus equipment itself is so humongous that it takes over 30 massive trucks to transport them to the next location.

There are over 25 families staying in this joint family of Kohinoor. Many of them are husband-wife duos. With both parents being performers, children pick up the ropes of circus from their infancy. Nay, from the time they are in their mothers' wombs. Like Abhimanyu.

The owner Amjad is a true patriarch who dotes on his family members, taking care of their every little need. To entertain these master entertainers, he has even installed a direct-to-tent television connection.

There were two gigantic goats moving around the circus tent that I mistook as circus performers gone astray. But Raja had an interesting story to tell.

Those two goats were bought by Amjad to be sacrificed on the day of Bakri Id. But during the entire week that these animals spent with him, Amjad had become so attached to them that he refused to sacrifice them on the appointed day. Now they go wherever the circus goes, as a constant reminder of Amjad's compassion.

With Raja's help, I met Pinki Khan, the multi-faceted star of the troupe. She in fact personified all that this amazing performing art stands for. She was charming and had tremendous presence; she had the svelte figure of an athlete; and she was a consummate performer. In short, she was the quintessential circus girl.

Pinki grew up watching her parents perform; and today she has taken over the mantle from them. She is equally adept at handling a slew of African parrots, or executing fabulous stunts on the bicycle, or performing the most breathtaking feat of them all: the flying trapeze. Her brother too is part of the troupe; he plays the keyboards in the circus band. Her husband has also been a part of the troupe for over seven years, and is today an accomplished trapeze artiste and an ace shooter. In short, they could easily be called the First Family of Kohinoor.

Pinki gets up at 5 in the morning every day and practises for five hours, just to be perfect. Because she believes that in a circus, you only get one chance. There is no retake.

Even today, after performing for more than a decade, she confessed she has an irrational fear running through her veins as she waits 80 feet above the ground waiting for the most awaited event of the show to begin: the trapeze. And every time it's her father, who's now the master trainer, who encourages her to take that all-important leap into the unknown.

Then I met Sagar Singh, a man who has been a clown for over 50 years. He's 75 now and still performs. Born in Purulia in West Bengal, he ran away from home when he was 12 to join the circus. The first job he got was to distribute pamphlets. Then he became an announcer going around on a cycle announcing the arrival of the circus. He was then taken as an extra in a minor item called the rope dance. He then graduated to become a motorcycle artiste, then a trapeze artiste, and then a trainer. But when there was a vacancy for a clown, he decided to take up that role permanently as that was what he loved the most. Make people laugh.

Once it so happened that he got a telegram when he was in the midst of a show. Since he was illiterate, he couldn't figure out what it said. He asked the manager to read it out to him. Just as he was informed that his son had died in a bus accident, the bell rang announcing his entry on the stage. In a daze he entered the ring and made people laugh with his antics, profusely crying under the thick make-up of a circus clown. After the show, he trudged back to the green room, accompanied by a deafening applause and then he fainted. This story travelled far and wide. So much so that Raj Kapoor the film maker came to meet him to hear this story. And inspired by it, he made the famous film 'Mera Naam Joker'. To this day, Sagar Singh is peeved by the fact that there was no mention of him, or his son, even at the very end of the long list of credits that came rolling down at the end of the film.

As I watched the finale of the circus, I saw Pinki's middle-aged mother perform on the swinging trapeze with consummate ease. And her father, the master trainer, kept an eagle eye on the proceedings to detect even a tiny flaw that could later prove fatal. And then came the climactic act of the flying trapeze. Perched high above mere mortals was Pinki, the lone girl among five other trapeze artistes.

My heart skipped a beat as she went flying on the trapeze, left it in mid-air, and then went gliding into the waiting hands of her partner.

That act for me symbolized the dying art of the circus. Here was a troupe of 250 hardworking and dedicated people, who, to keep the oldest performing art of India alive, have left the trapeze in mid air. With the fond hope that their outstretched hands will fondly and firmly be held by a discerning audience. Lest they fall into the bottomless pit of oblivion.

P.S. Just as the ink was drying on this page, I read a newspaper report about the artistes from Rambo Circus having performed in the renowned Prithvi Theatre of Mumbai on World Circus Day. This indoor show could well be the sign of things to come. And innovation may be the last hope for this performing art that has been slowly dying in this country in the last three decades. But I hope both versions continue to exist: the one in gigantic, magical tents and the one in small, discerning theatres.

the holy mess

Tungareshwar Wildlife Sanctuary adjoins Sanjay Gandhi National Park, the city forest of Mumbai. If SGNP is the right lung of this city, Tungareshwar is the left. But both lungs unfortunately are not in the pink of health. They are being choked with plastic that's the curse of mankind.

The waterfalls in Tungareshwar have dried up; and now only the memories of the last monsoon are flowing along the riverbed. When the waterfalls dried up, so did the picnickers. But they left behind tell-tale signs of copious consumption that will be an eyesore in these beautiful forests for another 300 years.

After the picnickers, came the devotees of Tungareshwar temple. They arrived in busloads for a recent puja. To keep their buses clean, they threw out the junk through the windows. To keep their bags clean, they discarded their waste in the bosom of Mother Nature. Yes, we have a strange concept of cleanliness. Anything outside of us, be it our house, our colony, or even our vehicle, is one infinite dustbin. And that sadly includes our beaches and our mountains and our forests, because we believe they are outside of us.

This eco-tragedy is at its most poignant during the Mahashivratri festival when Tungareshwar is at the receiving end. And so is Kanheri Caves in SGNP during the Buddha Pournima celebrations. Organisations like BNHS and other NGOs make valiant attempts at making sure the ecological damage is minimum. But then what is a handful of volunteers in front of a marauding crowd of a couple of lakhs?

As I gazed dejectedly at the litter of consumerism, I remembered a story about the Buddha. Once one of his disciples drew the Buddha's attention to the sad state of the disciple's robe. The Buddha promptly ordered for a new robe. Feeling a little guilty about his oversight, he went to the disciples's quarters in the evening to check if the robe fitted him well. The disciple said, 'Yes, master. It's very comfortable.' The master was curious to know what the disciple had done with his old robe. When he asked him, the disciple said, 'Sir it was in tatters, so I'm using it as my bedsheet.' The master then asked him what he had done with his old bedsheet, and the disciple said, 'Sir it was in real bad shape, so I'm using it as my floor mop.' When the Buddha asked where his old mop was, he said, 'Master, the mop was in shreds. So I am using the strands of the mop as wicks to light the lamps in your room.' Today, we would rush to the nearest Mall and buy a new gown, a new bedsheet, a new mop and new wicks. Because recycling is old hat.

To get away from this holy mess, and to enjoy the immense beauty of this sanctuary, there's only one way: Go where no one has ever gone before. And then you will start seeing flowers, moths, butterflies, spiders, reptiles, and birds of all colours, shapes and sounds.

The walk along a small stream was truly a mystical experience. On my left ear fell the murmur of the stream; and on the right ear birdcalls of different melodies. The two parts eventually merged in the core of my being with a divine stereophonic effect.

The issue of temples continuing to lie within the borders of Tungareshwar Sanctuary and Sanjay Gandhi National Park reminded me of a quaint little sanctuary in Wayanad in Kerala. It is called Janakikkaadu. When it was declared as a sanctuary, the settlements of the adivasis along with the temple of their tribal god were shifted out overnight. They meekly accepted it. And they left the temple behind and simply carried their deity away. To reinstall him close to their new home, and closer in their heart. Imagine the repercussions of moving the Tungareshwar Temple or the Buddha Temple out of their respective sanctuaries. It would create mayhem.

Maybe the lesser gods of tribals can easily be shoved aside, unlike the greater gods of mainstream religions. When will we realize that if one god can be relocated, so can the others be. Because all gods are created equal.

till the bisons come home

Radhanagari Sanctuary sits on top of Phonda Ghat at a gasping height of almost 4,000 feet. By the time the animals trudge up to the top, they must be thirsty like a crow. And that probably explains the existence of a plethora of waterholes here. Each one named after the animal that visits it the most. So there's Waaghaacha Paani or the Tiger's Waterhole, Sambar Kond or the Sambar Deer's Waterhole, and Geedhadaacha Paani or the Vulture's Waterhole.

The drive from the gate at Dajipur was 22 kms long and treacherous. The mud was loose and the stones were unreliable. At many points on the way, I had to ask everyone in the jeep to get down, so that the vehicle would become lighter and I could negotiate the climb better.

All along the journey into the forest we came across strange landscapes called sadaas. The first one was called Holicha Sadaa. These were massive bauxite boulders, jet black in colour, rising from the morning mist like prehistoric animals. Probably the name Holicha Sadaa came from the burnt look of these boulders, as if they had just emerged from a cosmic Holi.

At the next sadaa called Sawraicha Sadaa, there were tell-tale signs of an ancient seismic upheaval. There were large patches of salvadora here, a plant that's found only in mangroves. As also shells of dead snails scattered all along the table-land. Proving beyond doubt that all this was once upon a time under the sea, and in one massive volcanic eruption was flung high up onto these mystic mountains. And from the ever-soggy, moss-laden trees that were reminiscent of the dew-dripping trees of Cherrapunji, there sprouted exotic orchids from another land and another time.

The road to Sambar Kond was washed away in the last monsoon. As I walked on the road that didn't exist, a horde of inquisitive butterflies followed me to the waterhole. There, on a crisp carpet of dried leaves behind the ghostly trees, Kanta our guide heard some footfalls which he said were of a lone gaur or Indian bison. We waited with bated breath for a good 20 minutes, but the gaur refused to make its entry from behind the curtain of mist. It was only much later in the evening that we would lay our eyes on the largest of all wild oxen in the world. But when we did get to see it, we were convinced that few animals have the bucolic charm and the 12-pack abs of the gorgeous gaur.

On our return trip, I came across an artificial moat called saapla, made by the erstwhile King of Kolhapur, Shahu Maharaj. Once upon a time, not long ago, this moat used to be covered with dried branches, and hidden with dried leaves. Unsuspecting gaurs would be driven towards this trap by the beating of drums and clanging of cymbals. Once they fell into the moat they were shot dead at point-blank range, and their heads were then hung as trophies on the palace walls as a sign of the king's misplaced manhood.

When we reached the forest gate in the late afternoon, Kanta took us to his village Malaachi Wadi, with the promise of bisonspotting. There we saw the backwaters of a bund that served as a water source for the villagers, and as a waterhole for the gaurs.

It was apparently the most likely spot where gaurs would descend from the dense forests that enveloped the backwaters. We waited and we waited and we waited, but the gaurs didn't turn up for the appointment. Just as we started our trudge back cursing our bad luck, we heard a wild grunt that froze us in our track. Four majestic gaurs walked to the water's edge, and as they were lapping up the setting sun from the water, we crawled on all fours slowly towards them for a closer look. And in the darkness of the descending night, the aperture of my eyes were kept fully open, as also that of my camera. Just so that I could get two images that last a lifetime. One within, and one without.

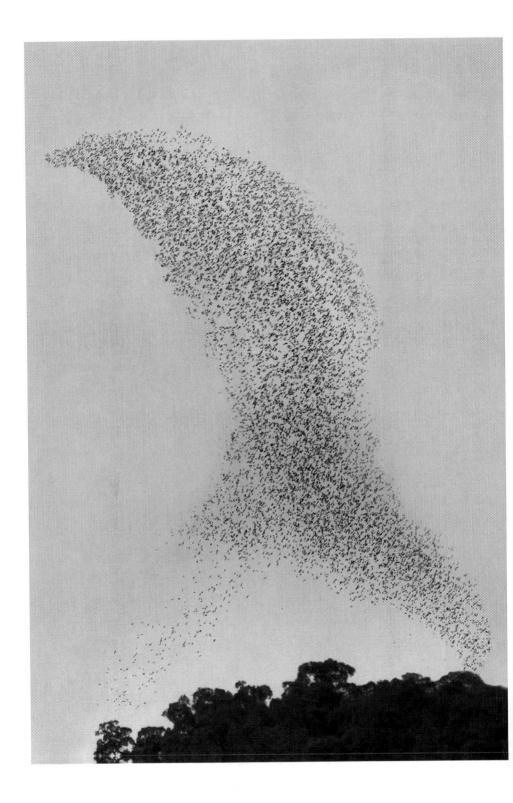

malaysia, once upon a time

When the plane descends into the State of Sarawak, the largest State in Malaysia, you indeed see a very large green cover. On closer inspection though, you realize green cover is not necessarily forest cover. The cover that you see here is of a plantation palm that's wreaking havoc in the rainforests of Malaysia: the oil palm. Being commercially viable, acres and acres of primary rainforests have been cleared in Malaysia to make way for this palm, the oil of which is exported the world over on a mammoth scale. Thus killing two trees with one axe: selling the priceless timber of trees that are many centuries old; and minting money selling the oil from the oil palms that have displaced them.

It's precisely this mindless destruction that Bruno Manser, the well-known and pioneering rainforest activist was fighting against way back in the 1990s.

Bruno, known as the Swiss Tarzan, lived with the nomadic Penan tribe for years documenting their life. He discovered that this shy and introvert tribe loves to stay deep inside the bosom of the forest with which they have been sharing a bond for 40,000 years. Extracting sago, which is their staple food, from the wild sago trees that are abundant here. And biting into the luscious durian fruit which is a delicacy they will not trade for the fruits of 'civilisation'. Once this food source starts getting depleted, they move on only to return to this patch after a decade by which time the forest would have replenished itself. To suit this nomadic lifestyle, their abodes are make-shift huts made in a hurry, as they are meant to last just a few months.

Another thing they love to do is hunt. They are masters in making blow-pipes and poison darts, and masters in hunting with them. The poison they use is extracted from the upas tree, or Antiaris toxicaria. And the dosage of the poison is meticulously calculated on the basis of the kind of prey.

The dense forests they dwelt in for millennia were invaded by the timber mafia in the 1980s who wantonly started felling thousands and thousands of trees that were hundreds of years old. This included the termite-resistant ironwood tree that is endemic to Borneo; as well as the durian tree, the seed of which takes as many as three years to germinate.

Bruno had adopted their language, and their customs, and lived like a Penan among them. So much so that they called him Lakei Penan or the Penan Man. They trusted him completely. When the timber mafia started making further inroads into their homeland, Bruno got hundreds of Penans to construct road-blocks along the mafia's path stopping them in their bloody tracks.

Much before Greenpeace activists thought of dramatic methods to get world attention, Bruno parachuted into the G7 Summit in 1992. He even hang-glided directly into the residence of the Chief Minister of Sarawak to seek his direct intervention.

But the government saw him as a rebel and arrested him twice. And both times he escaped and re-entered the forests of Mulu through the Indonesian border. He was last heard of in the year 2000, and then he mysteriously disappeared. It is widely believed that he was killed by the thugs of the timber mafia who saw him as a thorn in the bushes of the priceless rainforests. He was barely 46 years old then, and had a bounty of 40,000 USD on his conservationist head.

But Bruno Manser's death did not go in vain. It woke up the government of Malaysia to the smells and sights of their pristine rainforests; and in the last two decades they declared much of the rainforests that is left unscathed as protected. So now there are 27 national parks, 5 nature reserves, 5 wildlife sanctuaries and 32 protected forests in Malaysia.

Mulu National Park

When you reach Mulu, a UNESCO World Heritage Site, the plane lands bang in the middle of a rainforest. On all sides, for kilometres on end, there are endless stretches of dense, primary forests. Once upon a time, the whole of Malaysia would have looked like this. What is left now are small sanctuaries with an average size of just 3,000 hectares, and two large ones that average around 35,000 hectares. And these are completely cut off from each other, floating amidst degraded forests and concrete jungles.

But Mulu still contains as many 15 different types of forest harbouring 170 species of wild orchids, 10 species of carnivorous pitcher plants, 450 ferns, 4,000 fungi, 2,000 flowering plants and 20,000 insects. With many others yet to be discovered and given a name.

Our first foray into Mulu was the lovely trek to the Deer Cave. Part of the humongous network of caves that traverse the mystical mountains of Mulu, Deer Cave has the widest cave opening in the whole wide world. The mouth of this cave is kept open at an unbelievable height of 330 feet and a width of 300 feet. Inside there are millions of bats, their unmistakeable stench pervading the dark and moist cave. The caves in Mulu are acknowledged by geologists to have an evolutionary history that dates back 15,00,000 years.

At precisely 5.30 in the evening, we saw the spectacular sight of waves after endless waves of wrinkle-lipped bats coming out of Deer Cave, and flying to their feeding site 25 kms away. There were, hold your breath, 30 lakh of them, give or take a few thousands. They stream out of the cave every evening in a nonstop flow that lasts for all of three hours. Only to come back the next day at the break of dawn. It is said to be the largest exodus of bats witnessed anywhere in the world and perhaps the most awesome wildlife spectacle you can ever hope to see.

To reach the next set of breathtaking caves that was replete with natural sculptures, we had to take a longboat ride along the long-winding Melinau river. It felt like cruising down the amazing Amazon with enchanted rainforests on either side of the prehistoric river. As we hiked to the Cave of the Winds, we saw an entire rockface lined with a unique vegetation: the one-leaf plant.

This cave looked more like a series of cathedrals, one leading to the other. The impact of a gigantic river that once flowed through this cave was evident from the sudden twists and turns in the passage itself. This flow and the subsequent erosion have created a veritable art gallery of natural sculptures. These were tastefully illuminated, using footlights that were concealed behind other rockforms on the ground. One of the chambers was aptly named Queen's Chamber. It had limestone forms that looked like Corinthian pillars, thrones, ornate chairs, courtiers and chandeliers. In short all that would make up a queen's durbar. Another interesting cave in the mountains of Mulu is Sarawak Chamber. It is so massive that it can fit in London's St. Paul's Cathedral without a squeeze.

The nearby Clearwater Cave was even bigger in scale. Here the cave runs for 180 kms till you see light at the end of the tunnel. And for most of the stretch, 107 kms to be precise, a sub-terranean river gives it company. As on date, no man has ever traversed the entire length of this endless cave, end to end.

The last morning before our departure, we saw another strange happening: an entire grove of plantain trees with its flowers and fruits growing upwards. Our guide didn't know the reason why. Befuddled, we moved on.

Little did we know that at the end of the two km walk we will be seeing another breathtaking sight that'll stay with us till our last breath. Pedro the guide suddenly stopped at an innocuous wooden stairway in the middle of nowhere. It was the stairway to a green heaven. At a height of around 70 feet from the forest floor was a ropeway that extended for almost half a kilometre into the forest, giving us a hornbill's eye view of this mysterious forest. This secure, perfectly engineered marvel was stretched across mammoth trees that were at least a few centuries old. And as we looked up from the skywalk, we realized that almost two-third of the tree was still growing into the blue sky. Which meant that each of these trees were at least 200 feet tall. Close by, Pedro showed us a few belian, betang, tapang and kasai trees that were close to 800 years old. They stood tall, surveying the entire forest.

Standing atop the skywalk I peered into the towering branches of the gigantic trees. There, I wasn't looking for any of the 270-odd species of small birds or the 35 species of bats that are found here. I was looking for the most majestic bird of them all: the hornbill. A bird that somehow reminds me of the archaeopteryx though I haven't seen one yet. There was a reason for this eager search. And it was that Sarawak is called Bumi Kenyalang or the Land of the Hornbills. I would have been thrilled to spot any one of the 8 species found here. And I wasn't getting greedy and asking for the white-crowned hornbill or the helmeted hornbill or the rhinoceros hornbill. Even the most common among them would have sufficed. But neither here, nor anywhere else in the state of Sarawak, in the eight days of exploring the forests here, did we even get a glimpse of this imposing bird. Nay, we did spot one, and that was on the emblem of the Sarawak Tourism logo! Maybe I was plain unlucky, or may be the numbers have drastically dwindled due to fragmentation of forests, destruction of habitat, and the ritualistic obsession of the local tribes to collect the feathers and the beaks of hornbills to adorn their exotic headgear.

Leaving my disappointment behind, I continued my walk in that arboreal paradise. And that walk seemed like a walk in eternity. And I wished that it would never end. But then I realized, like Robert Browning much before me, that the woods are lovely, dark and deep, but I had promises to keep.

urban wildlife

On the descent from Udhagamandalam to Mysore, after 36 hair-pin bends and 38 kilometres of roads lined with forests, you come across Mudumalai Wildlife Sanctuary in Tamil Nadu. Situated in the Nilgiri Biosphere Reserve, it's at the cusp of three states: Tamil Nadu, Karnataka and Kerala. And adjoins three other wildlife sanctuaries: Bandipur, Nagarhole and Wyanad.

A century ago, Mudumalai and the nearby areas of Umbetta, Masinagudi and Kargudi were big-game reserves. After independence, a mere 320 square kilometres of Mudumalai was declared a wildlife sanctuary, leaving out vast stretches of dense forests in the three important areas adjoining it.

This made huge populations of wild elephants, wild dogs, hyaenas, gaur, sloth bear, leopards and tigers roam about in these unprotected areas that once belonged to them but have now been snatched away. Houses and farmhouses and farmlands have mushroomed in what was once the corridors of wildlife migration. Thus disorienting these helpless and hapless wild animals and scattering them across in eight directions.

Ombalan, a local wildlife expert, has witnessed dramatic changes in animal behaviour in the last decade alone. He said, 'Wild animals don't trust human beings anymore. How can they, when they have witnessed the brutal killing of members of their own herd by poachers? Or by reckless vehicles that speed along the national highway that slices this sanctuary into two?'

At his small, homely resort in Masinagudi, he showed me the amazing photographs and videos that he had taken in and around his resort that's a good eight kilometres before the sanctuary. There were tigers, leopards, wild dogs, elephants and sloth bear shot at various times in the year, over the years. As bed-time stories, he recounted how an Indian wildlife photographer survived an elephant attack two kilometres from his resort around four years ago, and how a French lady photographer was mauled and killed by a lone tusker at a place called Bokkapuram just four kilometres away, just last year.

Spending the night alone in the watch tower at the end of the complex and the beginning of the forest, I heard the creaking of the bamboos as they rubbed against each other in the breeze. It sounded like the doors of the forest were creaking open; and I imagined hordes of wild animals leaving the forest and coming and standing under the watch tower.

The next day, Ombalan drove me to Mudumalai. Near the reception centre of the sanctuary, I witnessed a heart-warming scene. There was a speed-breaker on the road as the centre was right on the Ooty-Mysore highway. A group of rhesus monkeys had strategically placed themselves near this speed-breaker, and as soon as tempos laden with fruits and vegetables inevitably slowed down here, they would quickly climb on to these vehicles and vamoose after stealing whatever they could lay their hands on. I wasn't sure whether it was lack of food sources in the forest that lead them to this lateral solution, or whether it was an easy, mischievous way to handpick your fruits and vegetables.

Taking the elephant ride from the centre, I entered the forest. Wildlife was conspicuous by their absence. It was almost as if they had deserted the forest en masse. Selvam the mahout took us to a salt-lick where we were almost certain to find some wildlife. And right enough there was a small herd of elephants there with five adults and two calves in tow. Selvam said, 'Sir, just a few years ago the average size of a herd used to be 25 to 30. Now it's come down to around 10.' And I remembered having read in a wildlife report that lack of sufficient food is one reason why numbers in a herd are dwindling. In fact in that report it was even observed that reduction in prey base has reduced the average weight and size of tigers across India over the last decade or so.

On my way back to the resort, Ombalan took me to the elephant camp in Theppakkad. Situated on the banks of the Moyar river, it was a centre for breeding and training elephants. These tame elephants, called kumkis in Tamil, are pressed into urgent service many times against their own wild brethren. To push them back into the forest when they stray into human settlements in desperation.

At the only photography institute in India, Light and Life Academy in Ooty, I was told about the endless 'intrusions' of wildlife into urban jungles. Iqbal Mohamad, the principal of this college, on an early morning drive saw a leopard as it leapt across just in front of his unbelieving car. Charan Hegde, the Head of Administration there, saw a hungry sloth bear on the roof of his bunglow as it was planning to cross over to the neighbour's house to steal honey from their apiary. And there was a news item in The Hindu about an ex army officer who was gored to death by a gaur in nearby Coonoor when he had gone for his morning walk.

All this made me wonder: Is it a case of man taking over the forests or is it wild animals taking over the urban jungle? Whatever be the truth, it is only bound to lead to unprecedented disaster.

the breathing stones

The stones that came to life here at the hands of the Pallava sculptors have been breathing for the last 1,500 years. And the stones that have just been given life by their descendants will be breathing for the next 1,500. That's the living tradition of an artistic land called Mamallapuram.

The whole village here is a World Heritage Site, and it has a small area of 8 sq kms and a miniscule population of less than 8,000. Around 200 of them carry forward the magical tradition of breathing life into stone. And in many houses you will find three generations of sculptors chiselling under one roof; their chisels falling on granite rocks in an inherited symphony.

It was at the sanctum sanctorum of the Shore Temple that I had the darshan of the best history teacher I had ever met. His name was C. K. Prasad, and he looked the most unlikely candidate for the job. He was well-dressed to a fault, and had a quiet presence that only comes with intense introspection. He was a retired civil engineer who lived in Chennai and who travelled 60 kms every day from there to Mamallapuram only because he was in love with this place. He didn't have a fixed rate for his services as a guide. He would be happy with anything that I gave him he said, simply because he would have done it anyway for free. Later I was to realize that he was an encyclopaedia of Pallava art and history, and I really wondered if he wasn't a descendant of a Mamalla king of yesteryears.

The Shore Temple was excavated by the British from the golden sands of Mamallapuram in the 1900s, but it went under the sand again in the dreaded tsunami of 2004. After the second excavation, 80 guardian Nandis have been lined up to form a protective ring around the sacred shivling here. But will they be able to protect the God of Destruction from the next tsunami? I wonder.

A unique feature of this temple is that the shivling here is so strategically placed that it is bathed in a golden sunlight, both at sunrise and sunset.

Situated bang in the middle of what was once a busy sea-port, it is considered to be the very first example of the finely evolved Dravidian style of architecture.

It is interesting to note that of all the temples in Mamallapuram, there's only one that's live: the Vishnu temple in the heart of the village. The others are all just architectural monuments: some rock-cut, some monolithic.

The most spectacular of the monolithic ones is Five Rathas. These are five temples in the shape of five chariots, each one carved in a different architectural style. Though they are named after the Pandavas, the deities inside are Vishnu, Shiva, Durga, Indra and Surya.

Then I saw an amazing cave with two dramatically opposite scenes enacted on either side of the cave. On the left was the gruesome scene of Durga slaying Mahishasura; and on the right was the tranquil, cosmic sleep of Vishnu reclining on the serpent Shesh Nag.

Behind this cave was the lighthouse of the Pallavas which was lit by a fireplace and not a lamp. To its right is the world's largest bas-relief sculpture measuring all of 100 feet by 40 feet, where the main narrative is Arjuna standing on one leg and doing penance in Kailas. The natural fissure in this massive boulder has been incorporated into the sculpture itself. So in monsoon the gushing water that flows through the fissure looks like River Ganga descending from Kailas to the Earth.

To the north of this man-made marvel is a marvel of nature. A huge boulder with a height of 35 feet so precariously placed on a slope that it looks like it could be toppled by the gentle push of a little kid. But village folklore has it that all the king's horses and all the king's men could not move it by an inch. For some strange reason, this humongous inedible rock is called Krishna's Butter Ball.

All these wonders in stone are sprinkled in a radius of just 2 kms. The only one that's away from here is a piece that should not be missed. It's on the Mamallapuram-Chennai highway, some four kms away, and is called the Tiger's Cave. This is an open-air theatre, and the stage is lodged right inside the mouth of a sculpted tiger. Next to the cave is a watchtower in the shape of an obelisk, from where on a clear day you could spot the enemy in the sea.

The many structures that are left incomplete here show that Mamallapuram was still work-in-progress, even after two centuries of nonstop chiselling. And the work couldn't be completed because the chisels of the Pallavas were silenced by those of the Cholas who captured their kingdom. But when the dust of the battle settled, a new style had emerged that was a blend of the Pallava and the Chola styles. A style that carried on the tradition of breathing life into stone.

Cholamandal Artists' Village: at a sculpted stone's throw

When the Pallavas were vanquished by the Cholas, the art too underwent a metamorphosis. The robust Pallava style was tempered by a more lyrical Chola style, the epitome of which is seen in the sculpture of the dancing Nataraja.

Inspired by this, K.C.S. Paniker, one of the precursors of modern art in India, established Cholamandal Artists' Village between Mamallapuram and Chennai on the East Coast. The idea was to have a community of artists living and working in the same place: Artists who wanted to break away from Western influences and search for a distinctly Indian idiom. The result was a style that was an amalgamation of imagery from tantra, motifs from yantra, mathematical symbols, Indian mythology, and even Indian calligraphy. All of which was witnessed in the Madras Art Movement for the very first time in Indian paintings.

When I walked into this idyllic art world, I was greeted by an affable lady who took me around. First to K.C.S. Paniker Museum of the Madras Art Movement and then to the two adjoining art galleries. But the open-air international sculpture park was a unique experience in itself. The sculptures here took on a different meaning altogether as they sprouted from the landscape like living organisms.

Yes, whether it is the traditional sculptures that are influenced by the Pallavas, or the contemporary sculptures that are inspired by the Cholas, every stone in Mamallapuram has a life of its own. Legend has it that once a sthapathi (or master sculptor) created an idol so full of life that when his chisel fell on the deity's hand, the hand started bleeding.

big cat diary

There's only one principle that I have followed in my 35 years of travelling into the wild: Never visit the same place twice. The simple reasoning is, there's so much to see in India you can't see it all in one lifetime. (Is that the reason why we Indians believe in rebirth, I romantically wonder.) Of course, I did make an exception once. That was Silent Valley in Kerala. I have visited this forest twice. Once as a 23-year-old to make an anti-dam documentary on this endangered forest. And then as a 53-year-old with my son and my wife to relive my nostalgia.

I felt it was time to make a second exception. For a tiger reserve called Tadoba. (Usually, big cats don't feature in my bucket list; even a flying lizard is enough to send me into raptures. But this time, the urge to spot the big cats suddenly overpowered me, and I decided to go there in the oppressive heat of 43 degrees C). On hindsight, it was a pretty good decision. Because it turned out to be the richest wildlife spectacle that I have witnessed in our amazing land.

Spread over 600 sq kms, Tadoba Tiger Reserve is an enchanting forest made up of three ranges that contribute in equal measure: Moharli, Tadoba and Andhari. And it is a supreme example of eco-tourism where the locals and the forest department do a wonderful job of protecting wildlife, and controlling close to a hundred congenitally vocal tourists every day.

21st April 2014

Day One. As we approached the buffer area of Tadoba, Mehar our sarathi slowed down at a village and pointed to a haystack where a leopard had climbed up to when he was caught stealing a calf in broad moonlight. He refused to be tranquilised in spite of two potent shots. And finally the villagers who had gheraoed the stack had to make way for the cat to retreat to the core area, his head still held majestically high.

After a hurried lunch we waited for the finest guide in Tadoba, Bandu, to pick us up. He arrived a second before 2.30 and we proceeded on our very first exploration.

Soon after entering the gate of the core area, we chanced upon a sloth bear. The glimpse was momentary as he was deep inside, foraging for termites in a distant mound.

Then we drove to a lake named Telia, which for some unknown reason had strange rainbow-coloured shores. Here we waited for a tiger spotted by another jeep three minutes ago. But no luck. And I realized that in Nature, just as in life, one has to be at the right place at the right time.

22nd April 2014

Day Two. Since most of the villages had been relocated outside the park long ago, there was not a single instance of cattle grazing. When the grass supply increased, the prey-base increased. And when the prey-base improved, the number of predators increased. Plentiful food, coupled with abundant water in all the water bodies, has made Tadoba a paradise for wildlife. The proof of the pudding was in the sighting. I saw bison, barking deer, chousingha, chital, sambar and nilgai, all in heartwarming numbers.

During my four-day stay in Tadoba, I didn't find any litter in the forest whatsoever. When our diligent guide Nilkanth did find one lone plastic bottle that must have been surreptitiously dropped from a jeep, he got down, picked it up, and quietly put it in our jeep to carry it back to civilization.

At Telia, on a small mound there were four peafowl and a peacock, sunbathing. Nilkanth suddenly spotted a slight movement in the grass. It was a leopard lying in ambush. The sharp alarm call of a spoilsport langur was enough to scatter the peafowl in all directions. The leopard slipped away into the grasslands with, well, a sheepish grin.

The wait at the nearby lake at Pandhar Pauni was cut short by swarms of flies that would land on the sweaty, exposed parts of your body. They didn't bite, they just stuck to your body and soaked in your sweat.

Bandu, our personal guide-cum-driver, was truly a son of the forest. At times he would stop the jeep and chat with langurs, bisons and even jungle fowl. Born and brought up in Tadoba, his instincts were finely honed. He set off to Telia again, guided by some sixth sense. On the way, he refused to stop when we spotted minor delights like birds and butterflies. Like a predator hunting its prey, his eyes were locked on a single target. And when we reached the lake, right enough there was a tigress cooling its heels in the water. After a full 30 minutes, she got up. And then slowly the drenched beauty walked towards us, and then turned and disappeared into the mystery of the forest.

The morning started with a leopard and the evening ended with a tiger. At the same lake. Busting the myth that leopards and tigers don't coexist in the same territory.

23rd April 2014

Day Three. On the way to Panchdhara, near Khatoda gate, we came across a large group of wild dogs that soon split into two groups to prepare for an ambush. A pack of wild dogs is so ferocious and merciless that it sends a chill even down a tiger's spine.

Then we saw two strange sights. A tree with as many as twenty-three beehives bustling with busybees. And a cluster of a tree called Ghost of the Forest. These trees are white in colour and on a moonlit night they rise above the forest like ghostly apparitions with their twisted arms outstretched. In one large patch there were around twenty of them; and I imagined what a sight it must be when they rise in eerie unison on a full moon night.

Mahua trees were in full bloom. When the mahua flowers and fruits fall down and fester, the langurs gather in large numbers to eat them. The fermented concoction gives them a high, and then they doze off in the shade till the effect slowly wears away. It's another matter that those who have had one fruit too many get up with a hangover.

We could now see Tadoba lake in the distance. Nilkanth shared with us the legend of this lake. Many centuries ago, a marriage party of the Gond tribe that used to inhabit this forest was passing through. Since their throats were parched and there was not a drop to drink, they decided to dig a well. Unfortunately when they dug they hit a rock in which a god resided. More than hurt, he was angry. And in a fit of rage, he sent forth a deluge of water that drowned the unsuspecting marriage party. All the water that gushed forth in anger formed the Tadoba lake.

The tryst with another tigress was in the evening. It was near an evacuated village called Jamni. As if from nowhere, she emerged and got on to the road in front of us. And apparently once a big cat decides to take the road to its destination, even if it's man-made, nothing can deter it. So, it passed by the two jeeps in front of us and came straight towards our jeep. And after giving a piercing look at the frightened eyes of my jeep, she passed by nonchalantly.

24th April 2014

Day Four. Only about 15 percent of the forest reserve is open to visitors. In the rest of the forest, the wild ways are unseen to man. And only 22 vehicles are allowed per trip, and every vehicle has to have a registered guide. All of them hail from the village and protect the forest like their own. They are knowledgeable, affable and willingly share information of various sightings with each other.

The last day of the trip was the best. It's on that day that I drove through the Tunnel of the Cicadas. The rest of the forest was silent; but as you approached this tunnel, the singing of cicadas slowly became louder. When you were right in the middle, the sound was at its peak. And as you exited the tunnel, the sound again disappeared into the distance.

Who was to prepare me for the stripes at the end of the tunnel? Just as we emerged from this reverie, on the left was Wagdoh, the alpha male tiger in these neck of the woods. Acknowledged to be the largest tiger in the country, he was a sight to behold. He was deep inside the bamboo grove, and gave us glimpses of his majesty through fleeting bamboo curtains. And then he disappeared suddenly. The fact that he wasn't seen again added to the ethereal quality of the sighting.

The next halt was Pandhar Pauni. When we reached there, we saw another tigress lying on the grass on the lakeshore, getting ready for a kill. Barely 50 feet away from her was a female sambar deer about to walk down into the watering hole. The alert deer suddenly noticed a faint movement in the grass as the tigress lifted her front legs and prepared for the big leap. And all of a sudden the sambar bolted with a sharp call that made even the wild boar and spotted deer disappear in a flash. Unmoved, the tigress got up and strode away as if nothing had happened. That's when I realised that Nature is perfectly balanced. The predator and the prey are equally camouflaged; and so are their instincts equally matched. Which is why a predator makes a kill only once in 20 attempts.

This tigress is fondly called Maya by the guides. And there's a strong rumour floating around that Maya is pregnant. Bandu gave that as the definitive reason why she didn't give the sambar a hot pursuit. The news of pregnancy warmed my cockles. Because, any new birth, of any species in the forest, is the surest sign of a forest in the green of health.